UNDERSTANDING CHINA

SUNY Series in International Management

Andrezj Kozminski, Patricia Sanders, and
Sarah Sanderson King, Editors

UNDERSTANDING CHINA

CENTER STAGE OF THE FOURTH POWER

YANAN JU

STATE UNIVERSITY OF NEW YORK PRESS

Published by
State University of New York Press, Albany

For information, address State University of New York Press,
State University Plaza, Albany, N.Y. 12246

Production by M. R. Mulholland
Marketing by Theresa A. Swierzowski

Library of Congress Cataloging-in-Publication Data

Chü, Yen-an.
    Understanding China : center stage of the Fourth Power / Yanan Ju.
        p.   cm. — (SUNY series in international management)
    Includes index.
    ISBN 0-7914-3121-5 (hc : alk. paper). — ISBN 0-7914-3122-3 (pbk.
    : alk. paper)
    1. China. 2. China—Economic conditions—1976–   3. China—
Social conditions—1976-   I. Title.   II. Series.
DS779.2.C4814   1996
951.05'9—dc20
                                                    95-52977
                                                    CIP
                                                    Rev

10 9 8 7 6 5 4 3 2 1

To China,
the land where I was born
and grew up with dreams.

Contents

PREFACE

China is becoming hot again. This time more among CEOs, investors, business brokers, traders, and entrepreneurs, rather than politicians or political statesmen like the late Richard Nixon, who made history by going to Beijing to shake hands with Mao. China was happy with Nixon, but now she loves Jack Welch or Hong Kong billionaire Li Ka-shing even more. Many of the early hardcore China enthusiasts, including those who had supported Mao's revolution until Deng took over, are finding themselves out of favor with Beijing. Later adventurers, people who came in the eighties or are traveling on the yellow earth now, would hear their Chinese hosts talk more about trade or investment opportunities than about the terracotta soldiers unearthed in Xian and the grandeur of the Great Wall. China is changing rapidly, and so are the Chinese—so rapidly that even the Chinese themselves can't quite follow the pace.

This book is an attempt to shed light on what's happening in China—or, more accurately, Greater China. It is *not* an economic assessment of this largest potential market of the world, though I have tried to convince my readers that China is becoming an important part of the global economy and it will be costly for businesses not to appreciate this. Nor is it a cultural study, though I have tried to analyze Chinese economic and political behaviors from a cultural perspective. As the reader will soon discover, this slim volume does not pretend to be a scientific study of the dynamics of the emerging Fourth Power, which is a larger category than Greater China. Rather, this book is the fruit of observations and reflections based on my more than three decades of life-experience in the People's Republic and my earlier work in contemporary Chinese studies.

In this book I will focus on issues and unanswered questions that people have been trying to understand in recent years: Is the Fourth Power real? To what extent will the Chinese economies—those of the People's Republic of China, Taiwan, Hong Kong, and Chinese family businesses in Southeast Asia and other parts of the world—change the landscape of the global economy? Why is it important to understand the way Chinese do businesses among themselves and with others? Is it culturally appropriate and practically meaningful to ask when China will have democracy? Can an economically booming China survive a systemically and morally corrupt China? What does the future hold for China? What is the most sustainable resource of the Fourth Power? The seven chapters are my answers to these questions. It concerns me less that I will obtain the full consensus or even partial agreement from readers than it is my hope that my perspectives, as those of an insider looking from the outside, can at least be used as an informed reference.

It would be misleading to call my perspectives "Chinese perspectives." I find it quite impossible to define so-called "Chinese perspectives." The individual views of Chinese on China are as diverse as in any culture. What makes the world of ideas and ideologies exciting is that individuals, be they Chinese or non-Chinese, see things from different perspectives. I would feel more comfortable simply calling my views the views of a Chinese individual, which may be representative of Chinese who share similar life-experiences under similar historical circumstances. I do not deny the strong possibility that my perspectives are biased due to the limitations that have been imposed on me by history. I am also keenly aware of the possibility that my perspectives may displease not only Western readers but also many of my fellow Chinese—such are the controversies revolving around contemporary China. Differences of opinion are healthy and can at times be beneficial.

On 6 August 1995, my friend Dai and I were walking down Mount Tai in China after our pilgrimage to the temples on the summit. For the first time in my life, I truly realized the truth: it is easier to climb a mountain than to walk down. It was steep. It was raining. It was slippery. And it was very dangerous. I felt scared. I am feeling the same way as I submit the final manuscript of this book to the press. I thought I was very brave when I decided to climb the mountain of China. Now I am at the mercy of my readers.

Had not been constantly encouraged by my long-time friend Professor Donald Cushman, I would have given up. Don, I finally made it. Thanks! My thanks also go to Linda Tomasso who helped me redefine the outer beauty of language and inner beauty of logic. I would like to thank Zhou Feng and Zhou Tong—both former graduate students whom I advised at Central Connecticut State University—for their help with the appendices.

1

Beijing: The Year 2000

As far as anyone can guess, it was around 1500 that Europe overtook China as the world's most advanced civilization. For centuries—maybe always—before then, Chinese science and technology and Chinese productivity and incomes were the world's best. Over the next 500 years, as the West grew rich and strong, China first lay torpid and then, for most of this century, was convulsed by revolutions, war, famine, Communist tyranny and a decade of anarchy called the cultural revolution. It may therefore come as a surprise that, just a generation from now, one of the world's weightiest questions may well be how to handle a self-confident nuclear-armed China presiding over the biggest economy on earth.

—*The Economist*, "China: The Titan Stirs"[1]

I was calming some visitors from the People's Republic of China: "This is not the end of the world. The year 2000 will still arrive in Beijing as it will in Sydney." As I began writing this book, International Olympic Committee (IOC) President Juan Antonio Sarmaranch announced Sydney to be the winner for hosting the Year 2000 Summer Olympic Games, beating Beijing and the three other bidding cities. A hysteria subsided on the yellow earth. A renowned Chinese fortuneteller who was reported to have predicted that Beijing would be the winner, became suddenly quiet. A nationwide reflection, like that which occurs after any major national victory or tragedy, began, albeit painfully, once again.

Failure of Olympic Bidding: A Good Lesson to Learn

If there was anything for the Chinese team to regret, among its bidding strategies, was the timing of the release of

China's most prominent political prisoner Wei Jingsheng.[2] The timing couldn't have been worse—to free Wei Jingsheng days before 89 IOC members voted to decide on the site of the Year 2000 Summer Olympic Games. Wasn't the move reminding a watching world that China did indeed have human rights problems and now we are letting this guy go? Wasn't it that you were telling the world we have jailed this man for more than fourteen years and now we need his release to improve our image? Wasn't this a deadly message? The man who decided to let Wei Jingsheng go should be awarded a medal for the World's Worst Public Relations Move. No matter how hard you tried to convince a calculating world of the coincidental timing of Wei's release, even diehard supporters of China had difficulty not relating the two events. Forget about Sarmaranch's announcement from Monte Carlo. Wei Jingsheng got out[3] anyway—connected or not with Beijing's Olympic bid—after more than fourteen years of confinement. Wei has paid and is still paying the price for what he did. And it may have been a price worth paying, probably less for China's democracy movement than for Deng Xiaoping's economic reforms, which began in the year of 1979 when Wei Jingsheng was thrown into jail. As tragic as Wei's and many of his colleagues' personal fates have been, Deng Xiaoping seems to be entitled to credit for China's booming economy, which has enjoyed an annual growth rate approaching double digits consistently over the past fourteen years, an economic miracle unheard of in history. History as human memories of the things said and done can be rewritten, and indeed historians are all rewriters of history, be loved or hated by later generations. History as the things that have been said and done, alas, is irreversible; no one can go back to 1979, for example, and rewalk the fourteen years by taking a different course. It's practically too late to ask "What if Wei Jingsheng had been freed fourteen years earlier?" "What if Deng Xiaoping had allowed more room for political reform?" "What if the Chinese had gone the Russian way?" These "what-ifs" and many others have little relevancy to a history forever passed, however recent it may have been. What cannot be changed is this: Wei Jingsheng spent more than fourteen years imprisoned; Deng Xiaoping succeeded in elevating China to be the center of an emerging fourth economic power after Japan, the United States of America, and the European Union. Who has been morally or practically right could be debated into the next century.

Beijing's defeat was a bitter defeat for at least 98.7 percent of the capital's residents who voted to support their city's bid for the Olympic Games 2000. Hold the tears; let's face reality. Even though the *New York Times* criticized the Chinese harshly in its 21 September 1993 editorial,[4] it was honest to say China's turn had "not yet" come. Not yet—probably not because of its human rights record. Not yet—definitely not because China's Great Wall or Beijing's Forbidden City lacked appeal for Olympic visitors. Not yet—probably not because of the fact that Sydney had a better infrastructure. Not yet—simply because many Western IOC members, a voting majority, nixed Beijing. Apparently these people were not sufficiently impressed when people who sympathized with the Chinese said China's 1.2 billion population deserved a chance. An arrogant *New York Times* editorial writer says "it will be time enough. But not yet."

The Chinese may have been unspeakably wronged this time. A peasant, simple as she may be, can distinguish being treated well from being treated without respect. People never seemed to have carefully read the messages implied in Beijing's almost hysterical bidding effort. First, this was the first time in the Olympic history that China, the most populous nation on earth, had ever applied for the right to host this prestigious, larger-than-sports event. China had never had the resources, the courage, or the right domestic political climate to do so. Second, this signified China's reformers' serious commitment to keeping the door of the nation wide open to the outside, and wouldn't this be a more solid and realistic development than for democracy fighters to make a dozen romantic requests for freedom? Third, never before had China, since the triumph of its Communist Revolution, been this sincere and eager and childishly naive in her effort to embrace the "blue ocean."[5] The Chinese infatuation with a maiden love with the larger world soon turned into a bitter embarrassment. Fourth, more importantly, China's next five years could be the last and one of the greatest economic miracles in mankind's most important century—the twentieth century—and this miracle is not only the miracle of China, but also the miracle of the Chinese. This is the miracle of the emergence of the Fourth Power. The end-of-the-century celebration of this miracle in the year 2000 in Beijing could be as big as the Summer Olympic Games in Sydney.

This would-be economic miracle should be more important to the Chinese than the city selected to be the site of Olympia 2000. The estimated over 5 billion U.S. dollars of business that the Games could bring to a host city pales when compared to the economic miracle which could develop in China over the next five years. This miracle is possible if existing and latent obstacles are removed along the way which will lead the Chinese to developing a Fourth Power that will compete against the United States, the European Union, and Japan, not for larger political influence, but for a larger share of the global economy. The U.S. Congress and the European Parliament were able to pass a resolution to denounce Beijing's Olympic bid, but they could do very little to block a consolidated Fourth Power from emerging from the horizon with its multicenter located in Beijing, Shanghai, Guangzhou, Hong Kong, Taipei, and other parts of China or beyond its borders within the East.

The defeat of Beijing's Olympic bid hurt the Chinese emotionally, but it was functionally good for China. It was good because it represented a bucket of chilly water splashed on a hot-headed bidding team. China needs to learn, next time, to be a bit more subtle and less opportunistic. It was good because China, over the next few years, needs to focus on her domestic issues and problems, its economy, and its own vast expanse of yellow earth. A yellow earth and a blue ocean are too different to be reconciled. But *when you are rich and powerful, not only will everybody, yellow or white, come to you, but they will make you the center of attention. It's never an issue of the color of skin, it's still less an issue of so-called clashes between civilizations as Samuel Huntington[6] suggests. It is an issue of haves and have-nots, that is, the classic issue of whether or not you have wealth and power.* The Chinese need to work hard to get rich and powerful to claim its world respect like Japan did in 1960 and South Korea did in 1984.[7] And only when China becomes sufficiently developed to give birth to a middle class, can the Chinese meaningfully talk about democracy, albeit a different kind of democracy than Uncle Sam's, or nobody will listen. When Wei Jingsheng was thrown into jail, who in China cared?

It was profoundly significant that a West-dominated IOC voted not to give the 1.2 billion Chinese the right to host the 2000 Olympics. It's a message that tells the Chinese to cool down and learn to treat themselves right: if you don't treat yourself right, shake off the shackles of poverty, and live in dignity, you should forever be ready to swallow the bitterness of whatever humiliation or embarrassment that may be visited on you. To quote again the *New York Times* editorial writer's words, "It will be time enough. But not yet." The Chinese, mainly the Chinese in the People's Republic, should now behave "with their tails tucked between their legs." They need to learn to "sleep on brushwood and taste gall," or *wo xin chang dan*[8] in Chinese, to constantly remind themselves that a poor and weak China wouldn't bring too much respect for the Chinese, not even Chinese in Hong Kong or in Taiwan, or elsewhere in the world. If you don't get the respect, it is not because you are yellow; it is because you are not rich and powerful. It sounds distastefully snobbish and cynical, but the world seems to function that way.

The bidding for the Olympic Games has been lost to Sydney, which well deserves it, but the year 2000 has not been lost to China. Beijing is not going to host the Games, but why not another kind of celebration, a celebration of the economic miracle that the Fourth Power will create over the next five years? What I am more interested in asking, however, is this question: What is this miracle going to look like? In view of what's happened in the past and what's happening now, let me make ten guesses in regard to what is going to happen in China by the year 2000:

Ten Guesses

1. *There will be laid a reasonably solid economic, financial, and technological foundation for the Fourth Power to emerge as the world's most formidable force ready to compete for a larger share of the global economy with the United States, Japan, and the European Union.* The Fourth Power, with its multicenter comprising at a minimum Beijing, Shanghai, Guangzhou, Hong Kong, and Taipei, consists of the economy of the People's Republic, the economy of Taiwan, the economy of Hong Kong, and Chinese family businesses in Singapore, Thailand, Malaysia, Indonesia, the Philippines, and other parts of the world. *The concept of the "Fourth Power" is purely economic and so is that of "multicenter." The background political system of each economic entity is irrelevant in this context. The Fourth Power is not a planned integration of the Chinese economies and businesses, nor is it a conspiracy for the Chinese to compete against non-Chinese. This is a natural convergence of economic powerhouses very much dictated by economic logic and a common cultural/business framework that all Chinese can comfortably identify with.* Unlike the European Union or the North American Free Trade Agreement (NAFTA) or the Asian Free Trade Area (AFTA), there will, and indeed could be no formal organization or agreement designed to hold this power together or forcibly break it up. Mainland China and Taiwan, for example, will still be far apart, but their economies will have been integrated to a degree much greater than now. Neither cultural goodwill nor political narrow-mindedness could promote or prevent such an integration as effectively as the internal economic logic and a shared cultural/business framework. In this sense, the final emergence of the Fourth Power will have been the result of this economic logic and common cultural/business framework; politics will have little role to play in the process.

The concept of the Fourth Power seems to be comparable with such economic entities as the North American Free Trade Area (NAFTA). But they are different. Whereas NAFTA or the European Union is regional and political in addition to economic, the Fourth Power is economic and cultural in the sense that the driving force of its formation has little to do with regionalism and protectionistic politics. If a Hong Kong businessman sees trading with Americans as having a higher chance of generating profit, he would probably go and trade with Americans. Now he goes to China to trade; the theory may well be that trading with China is easier and more attractive for him—easier and more attractive both economically and culturally. It is interesting to note that the Beijing government has refrained, in their official language, from the use of such terms as "the Fourth Power" or "Greater China," presumably out of fear that the United States, the European Union, Japan, and other non-Chinese economic entities might interpret such concepts as implying a conspiracy. Such fear is well taken but unnecessary. And it is pointless to suppress or even discourage academic discussions on the notion of "Greater China" or "the Fourth Power."

2. *The driving force of the Fourth Power will undoubtedly be the Chinese mainland, as dictated by economic logic.* Simply stated, this is going to be a place to put money in order to make money, whether or not you like, for example, such terms as "socialist market economy." The centripetal force of the yellow earth will have pulled the so-called periphery even closer toward Guangzhou, or Shanghai, or Beijing, or any other parts of the yellow earth. China cultural theorists such as Harvard professor Tu Weiming seem to believe that what is going to happen is the encirclement of the cultural center, which is mainland China, by forces on the periphery. Whether the center pulls the periphery or the periphery encircles the center depends on where you stand. What matters in the practical sense is that the center stage for the Chinese economic show will be the mainland. The International Monetary Fund (IMF) recently used purchasing-power parities (PPP) instead of market exchange rates to lift China's share of world output to 6 percent—three times its previous weight, making it the world's third largest economy behind the US (22.5 percent) and Japan (7.6 percent). The IMF's revised PPP-based weights put China's 1992 GDP at $2,000 billion ($1,700 per head). The World Bank estimated

that China's GDP was $2,210 billion in 1990 on a PPP basis. If two years of 10 percent growth and dollar inflation were added, this would suggest China's GDP could have reached $2,870 billion in 1992 ($2,460 per head). That makes the China of today the world's second largest economy. What will happen in the year 2000 if China keeps its annual growth rate at 7–8 percent in the next five years, which is not unlikely, and assuming that Japan and the United States will register a 2–3 percent annual growth rate? That means the size of China's economy will have become something that few players in the global economy can afford not to take seriously.

The economic miracles that two of the four Asian economic tigers—Taiwan and Hong Kong—have achieved are impressive. There should be little doubt that Taiwan's international trade experiences and manufacturing and management capabilities deserve serious study by mainland Chinese. It is a shared consensus among China's economic planners and financial officers of various industries that Hong Kong is a world-class leader in banking and finance and its time-honored business institutions are going to be a national treasure after the colony is returned to the People's Republic in 1997. Singapore, which is three-quarters Chinese, has been enjoying a fast-growing economy, a world-class telecommunications network, a stable government, a strong Confucian tradition, and a reasonably happy people. Taiwan, Hong Kong, Singapore, and Chinese who live in other parts of the world have been pressuring their compatriots on the mainland ever since the People's Republic opened its door in 1979. However, this does not change the size and strength and potentialities of China with a 1.2 billion population and an area larger than that of the United States. The Great Wall is still in China. The Yellow River is still in China. The vast majority of Chinese still live in China. The collective urge to get rich is stronger in China than anywhere else in the world. China, not the periphery, will be the main driving force of the Fourth Power.

3. *Peripheral-based Chinese will be key players in lifting Greater China to the status of the Fourth Power within the global economy.* Here I refer to the 55 million overseas

Chinese (including those of Taiwan and Hong Kong just for the convenience of grouping). Their capital, their market experiences, their managerial skills, and above all, their entrepreneurial spirit will play a key role not only in the economies of Taiwan, Hong Kong, Singapore, and various adoptive countries such as Thailand, Malaysia, Indonesia, and the Philippines, but also in the continuously booming economy of the People's Republic. Overseas Chinese will find doing business easier with their Chinese counterparts in China than non-Chinese will. This will be due largely to their following a common cultural/business framework, the explication of which will be the task of chapter 3. Overseas Chinese money will have flowed and continue to flow in large quantities with an accelerated speed into Guangdong, Fujian, Zhejiang, Shanghai, Jiangsu, Shandong, Hebei, northern China, and, gradually, into the less developed interior of the country. Meanwhile, non-Chinese companies and investors, mainly Americans and Europeans, will cooperate with overseas Chinese and depend on their sophisticated use of the common cultural/business framework to do business in China.

Hong Kong, due to its proximity to prosperous Guangdong Province and its scheduled return to China on 30 June 1997, has been investing heavily across the border and far into China's inner lands. Taiwan has become the second largest foreign investor in China after Hong Kong despite a sometimes quiet and sometimes quarrelsome political climate across the Taiwan Strait. Taiwan's trade with the mainland surpassed 16 billion U.S. dollars in 1994, and they are at this writing each other's fourth largest trade partner. Money and commodities do not travel alone. They come to the People's Republic along with human experiences, skills, and capabilities. Such human experiences, skills, and capabilities, which have come from the periphery, have been playing a key role in China's booming economy aided by an increasing volume of overseas Chinese investment.

4. *While Japan will never loosen its operations aimed at the potentially vast Chinese market, and Europeans will want to catch up, the Americans' love affair with China, first begun*

in the early 1980s, will be rekindled. The American example will illustrate how economic logic represents, in the final analysis, a more powerful force than political maneuvering on the part of the United States or China itself. It is the economic logic, or rather, the market force, that will pull aggressive and, in some cases, struggling, American companies toward the vast yellow earth behind the Great Wall. I heard employees of General Electric relate CEO Jack Welch's warning to them: you can't play big if you don't play with China. GE and other American giants are already on the move. At the time of writing this beginning chapter in early 1993, GE had received an $150 million order for aircraft engines. In addition, Jack Welch was looking for sales in power-generation equipment, locomotives, medical equipment, plastics, and electric lighting. Early in 1993, Aspen, Colorado–based Wing-Merril agreed to invest $2 billion in one of the biggest power projects in China, and will own 70 percent of the equity, something that could hardly occur ten years ago. AT&T, Boeing, Motorola, Coca-Cola, Arco, and other U.S.-based multinationals have increased and will continue to reinforce their presence in the world's potentially largest market. AT&T early in 1993 made a deal with China to make switches, advanced integrated circuits, and wireless phones, and this deal would, according to an AT&T official, "dwarf everything else AT&T does in the world." *Business Week* in its 29 March 1993 issue quoted Wing-Merril chairman John B. Wing as saying, "China is going to be a big global player, and if Americans aren't part of it, we are fools." It would be much more informative to watch where these seasoned business moguls move money to than to listen to a dozen slick politicians talk about a new world order. I would guess that by the year 2000 few Americans will claim they understand China and the Fourth Power better than people like Jack Welch and John Wing. Not self-styled China watchers, definitely not short-sighted politicians, not ardent China lovers, not even scholars specializing in Chinese studies. People who understand present-day China well are those who understand economic logic.

But accomplishment of anything good entails many twists and turns, as a popular Chinese saying goes. Relations between China and the United States have always been that way since they resumed normalcy in the early 1970s. The trade friction over the protection of intellectual property rights that erupted in early 1995 was just one of the most recent examples. There have been speculations about a possible trade war between the two trade giants. There is nothing inexplicable involved in this on-and-off, off-and-on friction between the two countries: they both love and hate each other for all conceivable reasons. But over the years, and particularly in recent decades, both have learned that they will fare better to love than to hate. In the final analysis, regardless of whether they are alternately amorous or hateful, they need to work their problems out as fast as they arise. It is politically short-sighted to see the current relational dynamics tipping more favorably toward the Chinese side. Visionary corporate leaders such as GE's Jack Welch do not see things that way. Politics put aside, neither China nor the United States can afford to neglect the other given the nature of their economies—both are becoming, albeit in different ways, increasingly interdependent upon each other and the rest of the world.

5. *China's infrastructure will improve, probably not as fast as the country's economic growth, but will attain a level unprecedented in China's history. This infrastructure consists of two parts: the material side and human component.* The material part includes highways, railroads, improved seaports, air transportation, and telecommunications. The human component will be composed of a new breed of CEOs, managers, bankers, investors, financial analysts, computer programers, engineers, marketing experts, consultants, and public relations agents.

By the year 2000 the whole of Asia will spend a total of $1.9 trillion on infrastructure. Among the biggest spenders are mainland China, Taiwan, and Hong Kong. For example, China alone will spend as much as $968.4 billion on transportation, $54.0 billion on power, and $25.2 billion on telecommunications. In comparison, Taiwan's figures are $124.3 billion, $28.5 billion, and $9.6 billion respectively. Hong Kong's projected spending of a total of $36.0 billion on transportation and telecommunications is also impressive.[9]

Shanghai, the largest commercial city in China and the most important political base for President Jiang Zemin and his protégés, is a typical example of how China has been struggling with a need to improve its infrastructure, a need that has never been felt so strongly since Deng began his economic reforms in 1979. Just ten years ago, I had my first home phone installed, and that was a rarity even for a professor. Today most of my colleagues and relatives have private phones, an unbelievable achievement for the telecommunications industry. But the waiting list for new phoneline applications is quite long in Shanghai, even though the installation fee has been increased to an exorbitant 5,000 yuan (about an average worker's annual wage!). When I first visited Shanghai in December 1993 after five and half years of absence, it had not changed too much in its road system, and the traffic was worse than in any large metropolitan city in the world. A year later, I returned to find the city's Beltway in use. I was impressed by the speed of construction, but disappointed to find little obvious improvement in its congested traffic situation. There have been constructed, in the past five years or so, two world-class suspension bridges over the Huangpu River connecting old downtown Shanghai and the city's new development zone, Pudong. While the two bridges add transportation capability to an already existing Yanan Road Tunnel going under the Huangpu River, they are far from sufficient in easing the traffic pressure on both Pudong and Puxi's (the old Shanghai part) economic development. This is typical of what's been happening in China's infrastructure: it is so hungry and so big that you can never feed it enough. It's been reported that Shanghai hopes to spend about $100 billion on the infrastructure of the city including Pudong by the year 2000. The appetite is big. The issue that is yet to be solved is where all this money will come from.

The human component of the infrastructure may well prove an even more exciting and challenging task. There should not be too difficult to find one hundred, one thousand, or even ten thousand world-class scientists in a country as large as China. And the availability of labor, including educated labor, presents little worry given the size of its population and nationwide compulsory primary and junior middle education. The challenge lies in the training of millions upon millions of qualified professionals who serve as the heads and backbones of organizations and of mediators whose task is to ensure a healthy execution of social contracts as the economy undergoes transformation from a planned system to one based on market mechanisms. I don't think it will hurt if professional trainers are invited from Hong Kong, Taiwan, or the West, but the ideal trainers will be the mainland Chinese themselves, for they understand the unique communication codes (not just the natural language) and, most importantly, possess a better and more intimate knowledge of all the contextual factors such as rules regarding political game playing, market needs, and the way people interact with each other on a daily basis. I have personally been involved in a number of Western-sponsored training programs designed to instruct business leaders and managers from the People's Republic. While they all played a certain positive role, they were, in my judgment, insufficiently effective due to a number of factors. First, the majority of such training seminars tended to treat no more than the basics, things that the Chinese could get from any bookstore. Second the majority of trainers had little knowledge of their audiences in terms of their academic and practical backgrounds. Third, there was little connection between what the trainer lectured on and the realities of Chinese business. Fourth, perhaps the biggest problem was the lack of well-qualified translators who not only speak both languages but have reasonable knowledge of the subject matter. But there seemed to be one big gain for those seminars that were conducted in the United States or other Western countries: trainees could get exposed to an exciting foreign culture and, more often than not, had a good time sightseeing.

I am always of the opinion that for China, with its different language, where the culture differs so much from the West, where the social and organizational reality can be so complex, and where the number of people that need to be trained is so large, you cannot not ignore the central importance of your own training resources. It is largely misinformation, this idea that China lacks first-class trainers of professional managers. My guess, which is very much based on personal observation and years of first-hand experience working as a management trainer in China, is that China has quite an army of qualified trainers who are capable of doing first-class work. Shanghai Industrial Consulting Company, for example, is one of many well-qualified training organizations in China whose management consultants and trainers may have a more intimate knowledge of Chinese industries, businesses, and markets than anyone else in the world.

6. *I will bet that China's political reform will be slow and reluctant and painful if there will be such a thing at all. Democracy will remain a luxury for the Chinese.* Benevolent authoritarianism will characterize China's political system probably for a long time to come. When it comes to the issue of political reform in China, different factions and interest groups, conservatives and liberals, in Beijing or at lower levels, will immediately become one and join together to limit political reform as much as they possibly can. The best argument, as it has always been, will be the necessity of preserving a stable environment within which to carry the economic reform further. This is indeed the most difficult dilemma the Chinese will face in the next five years and far into the twenty-first century. It is very true that a nation of 1.2 billion people needs stability. If one-tenth of the population, for whatever reason, flee China, wouldn't it be a disaster for its surrounding neighbors? Wouldn't it be a disaster for the whole world? Whoever argues against a radical political reform agenda using this logic will get sympathy because the risk is real and it is a sound argument. Therefore, whoever promotes political alternatives must be stopped or suppressed, resorting to whatever means. If we take a closer look at reality, even politically insensitive people would agree that the real resistance does not come from a shared perception that too fast a political reform would bring instability to society, which, whether you like it or not, is a valid argument. The real resistance comes from an unwillingness on the part of power-holders, probably more at lower levels than at higher levels, to give up the political resources at their disposal. Such political resources, in a rule-by-man-is-

larger-than-rule-of-law environment, can easily turn into commodities or cash or whatever form the power-holder wants as long as it's a "good" deal. In the next five years, China will still concentrate on its economy and the systemic reform in the economic field. But the deeper the economic reform goes, the louder the voices will be calling for political reform. While the political reform, no matter how hard the West tries to influence the political process in China as they have been doing in Russia, will not lead to the creation of a Western type of democracy, the People's Republic, nevertheless, would face an increasingly heightened pressure not necessarily from political activists like Wei Jingsheng, but a slowly growing middle class which may, little by little, want to have their voice heard. Such pressure may also come from the demands of a deepening and yet slowly progressing economic reform. Like the sun rising gradually from the east or slowly setting in the west, no one can stop the process. This process, nevertheless, will be slow and painful, and frustratingly unpredictable. Whether China will have democracy or be ruled by benevolent authoritarianism is the topic of chapter 4.

The widely shared perception that China's post-Deng period will be unpredictable feeds speculation among China watchers and media people. When Zhou Beifang, former chairman of Shougang Concord International Enterprises and Shougang Concord Grand—two of China's Capital Iron and Steel (called *Shougang* in Chinese) Corporation's five listed companies in Hong Kong—was arrested on corruption charges in mid-February 1995, some very different meanings were read into the unusual arrest. Some read it as a sign that China was starting to take corruption problems seriously. Others said this was a signal of Deng's waning power as he was nearing his death, on the theory that Zhou had close connections with Deng's family. Zhou's father, Zhou Guanwu, who resigned as head of the Capital Iron and Steel Corporation just before his son was arrested, was a good friend of Deng's. Such stories will proliferate, and the resulting speculations could be still wilder. Questions like the following will get repeated many times: Will Party Chief Jiang Zemin stay on top of the power hierarchy? Is Qiao Shi, now president of the People's Congress, a real blackhorse? What is going to be Li Peng's role after Deng dies? Will a civil war erupt even before Deng is gone? Who now controls the army? Will there be more or less democracy in the post-Deng era? To be honest, I, as a Chinese national who cares as much about China's future as most serious China watchers, have rarely asked myself these questions. It is not that I am not interested in the dynamics of Chinese politics. Rather, I have already decided, for myself, that China's road to its political future has pretty much been set; who will stay on in the power structure and who will go after Deng dies is not as important as whether or not the economic reform will continue and whether or not China is blessed with continued economic prosperity.

7. *Consumerisim, which has been on the rise in the past few years, will reach a new high by the year 2000.* When 1.2 billion hungry consumers buy, they will buy a lot, and when they buy a lot, they can buy everything up. Twenty years ago, the big three items on a Chinese family's "dream" shopping list were a wristwatch, a bicycle, and a sewing machine. Ten years ago, they became a color television set, a refrigerator, and a washing machine. Now they are a personal computer, a telephone, and perhaps a motorcycle. By the year 2000 will they be substituted by a family car or an electric motor-scooter? Chinese consumerism, like a person locked in a dark room for too long and finally exposed to dazzling sunlight, cannot make sense of what's going on and just wants to grab everything. Due to decades of controlled supply of consumer products and a strict rationing policy, mainland Chinese had learned to suppress their desire to consume, which was then considered a virtue. This has become history. Consumerism has become a new cultural value and has taken on ritualistic dimensions; it is now a daily routine for millions upon millions of hungry Chinese consumers. McDonald's, Coca-Cola, and Levi jeans have proved much more effective than the Voice of America and other Western propaganda machines in persuading the Chinese to go global. Benjamin Barber in his "Jihad vs. McWorld" in the March 1993 issue of *The Atlantic* discusses two opposing

trends of tribalism and globalism in the present-day world. By the year 2000, China will become a key player in McWorld, and the unavoidable jihad, or quasi-jihad, between Beijing and outlying localities, between the more developed coastal areas and the resource-rich but skill-poor interior provinces will not be holy wars fought out of varied "faiths," but fierce competitions for a larger piece of the McWorld pie. The 1.2 billion hungry consumers will need a very big piece to eat.

Let's play a little guessing game here. In the United States, after a home the most expensive single item that an average adult American must spend money on is an automobile. What will this item be in China around the turn of the century? Also a car? Not likely. My guess is a motorcycle or motorscooter. As is known to all, China is currently the kingdom of bicycles. In Shanghai alone, for example, there are 7 million registered bicycles. Are the Chinese dreaming of owning a car like Americans or Japanese or their compatriots in Taiwan or Hong Kong? There are such dreamers, but they represent only a tiny percentage of a population of 1.2 billion. A car is far too expensive for the average Chinese worker, whose annual income is no more than 1,000 U.S. dollars. "But can I, in my lifetime, enjoy the 'luxury' of riding a moped or motorscooter? Can I one day put down my bicycle that I have pedaled for so many years?" Many of my former colleagues, friends, and relatives are telling me they are asking these questions. Imagine this: what is likely to happen when the 7 million bicycles of Shanghai are, one day, replaced by other means of transportation? How many mopeds and motorscooters will be needed in that market? Shanghai represents about one percent of the country's population. Then how many mopeds and motor scooters will have to be manufactured and sold in the People's Republic? Based on this logic, I expect a booming market and the fiercest competition among moped and motorscooter manufacturers. By the turn of the century, China will be home to the world's largest concentration of motorcycles, mopeds and motorscooters.

8. *Pandemic corruption in China could prevent the consolidation of the Fourth Power by the year 2000.* High-ranking Chinese Communist Party officials have repeatedly warned

that the rampage of nationwide corruption may not only give the Party plenty of rope to hang itself but also bury all the hard-won fruits of the economic reform. Corruption is real and serious in China, but Chinese are no more corrupt than non-Chinese in other parts of the world. Moral corruption—corruption caused by social, political, or professional demoralization—is everywhere, in underdeveloped as well as developed countries. Structural corruption—corruption caused by structural instability in the political system, the lack of an institutionalized legal system, a continued, inequitable distribution of social wealth—is typical of a society undergoing major systemic transformations such as China, Russia, and many Eastern European countries. If engulfed by structural as well as moral corruption, the problem will assume nightmarish dimensions. It is by no means an exaggeration to say that a large portion of the 1.2 billion people are living in this nightmare. China's continuous economic boom and continuous improvement in people's living standards could help the Chinese walk out of this nightmare. However, the elimination of structural corruption would depend very much on reforms in economic, legal, and overall social structures, and on the building of a whole new generation of well-educated and well-disciplined cadres, while the key to the lessening of moral corruption seems to lie in a long and carefully designed civic educational program. Mere punishment or even frequent resorting to such harsh punishment as summary execution would not solve the problem. A corruption-ridden ailing China needs mental and bodily recuperation using traditional Chinese medicine as well as Western surgical operations. I guess the Chinese will have finally reached this consensus by the year 2000. The often asked question of "Can an economically booming China survive a systemically and morally corrupt China" will be answered in chapter 5.

9. *China's educational system holds the key to the future of China, and with it lies the future of the Fourth Power.* The kind of recuperation and healing that China needs will be conducted through education. Here I am talking about two kinds of education, moral education and science-based edu-

cation. After over four decades of social revolutions including the 1966–76 Cultural Revolution in which many traditional as well as more modern moral values were eradicated, China today is very different from the China of 1919 when there was an intellectual debate on whether or not democracy and science should be developed to save a sick young republic. *The China of today needs, I believe, morality and science. Democracy, Western type or Eastern type, could lead to chaos or become a fake if it is not built on a solid economic and moral foundation.* I am not against democracy, but democracy is not as urgently needed as morality or science at least for the next five years or so. Who then is going to be the most effective moral educator of a 1.2 billion people? Not the state, though it could help. Not the *danwei* (the Chinese term for "working unit"), though it must be supportive. Not religious leaders since religion has never been an important part of the life of an average Chinese (I wonder if there exist any influential religious leaders in present-day China). Not even schools, though they should play the role of moral reinforcer. The most effective educator of morality may be the nation's real or legendary models (such as the late Party Secretary Jiao Yulu of the Lankao County Committee, Henan Province) on the one hand, and individual Chinese families, nuclear or extended, on the other. We all know models educate. Here I want to stress that moral education could most effectively be carried out for family members by family members within the family. The reason is that family is probably the only social institution existing in China which has survived relatively intact the wars, revolutions, and political upheavals since the overthrow of China's last feudal dynasty in 1911. The Chinese family and moral values associated with family are still rock solid while Chian's cultural "Great Wall" is very much in ruins, waiting to be reconstructed.[10]

Science suffered greatly during the Cultural Revolution and has zigzaged since the economic reform started in 1979. Practitioners, not scientists, have benefited most in the past decade. Professors, scientists, scholars, and other elite intellectuals must be so well rewarded that they will all stay "home" instead of *xiahai*[11] or moonlighting to make a few yuan to make both ends meet. If, for example, a college professor in China continues to be paid a mere fraction of a Hong Kong professor's salary, China's dream of making the twenty-first century a good century for the Chinese will be cheap talk. It is not that China cannot afford to pay its elite intellectuals this much. Rather, China cannot afford not to "buy" Mr. Science and keep him on the job, happy and productive. If China continues to lose its best brains to a more competitive overseas job market, its continued growth cannot possibly be sustained beyond the year 2000. Why and how education holds the key to China's future is discussed in chapter 6, and why family is crucially important for China and the Fourth Power is the topic of chapter 7.

10. *China, despite all her blessings, has one deadly curse. And this deadly curse, paradoxically, is contained in one of the greatest blessings for her and for the whole world. This curse is not alleged violations of human rights or lack of democracy. This curse is not poverty. This curse is not intractable problems in the educational system. This curse is not even mass-scale social demoralization. These problems, thorny as they are, are solvable, however long it may take. This curse is its 1.2 billion population.* True, 1.2 billion consumers would be the world's greatest blessing from a market point of view: if each and every one of a 1.2 billion people buys a Nike, where else would Nike need to go to sell its shoes? Imagine one-tenth of the population becoming truly middle class and having money to shop with. Doesn't this translate to an attractive 120 million shoppers? How about 5 percent of the population riding motorcycles or motorscooters? Isn't 60 million a good number? But what about the remaining 1.08 billion or 1.14 billion? Don't they also need food, clothing, shelter, medical care, education, and jobs, if not a motorcycle? Suppose I have 10,000 workforce in my factory and I need only 3,000 and I must let the other 7,000 go. A rational conclusion, but where to let them go? Isn't it insane for a university to keep 5,000 teaching and administrative faculty for handling no more than 10,000 students? But the president of the university is dead meat as soon as he acts to prove himself a clear-minded, sense-making person. It

is sadly true: with a population as large as 1.2 billion, you cannot possibly think or act "normally"; you are cursed to think and act in what I call the Population Explosion Complex (PEC) way, no matter how abnormal or insane it may appear. Unfortunately, all mainland Chinese will have to share this abnormality. I wish to make it very clear at the very beginning that the emergence of the Fourth Power or the world's potentially largest market in the Orient does not imply in the least that an average Chinese mainlander will live as well as those who happened to be born in a resource-rich but population-problem-free social environment. The average Chinese will live a very modest material life by the year 2000, probably not even close to the kind of life that a lower-middle-income person leads in a developed country. This being said, however, the Fourth Power is still the Fourth Power. *Here is also involved an important point for all China watchers: always keep in mind China's explosively difficult population problem.*

Nicholas D. Kristof, in his article "China in the Year 2000," developed three scenarios based on real characters and settings that he came to know during his nearly five years as the *New York Times* bureau chief in Beijing.[12] After a sensational presentation of each of the three possible political states for China by the year 2000—an authoritarian dictatorship, "the emergence of a prosperous quasi-democracy," and a third scenario of "civil war and vast upheaval"—he asked: "Which scenario is most likely?" Cautioning that "predictions about China often end up more embarrassing than insightful," Kristof said he leaned toward the likelihood of a prosperous quasi-democracy. I find this difficult to accept. As 1.2 billion people advance toward a new century, I expect to see some kind of chaos, a controlled interregional chaos. Civil war and vast upheaval are more likely to occur in some republics of the former Soviet Union, probably including Russia, but not in China. There will be no democracy or quasi-democracy in China by the year 2000 either; the Western notion of democracy will continue to be alien to the Chinese government and its people. If democracy is compared to cereal and milk for breakfast, then 90 percent of the Chinese, at least in the next five years, would rather eat rice soup and rotten beancurd even though they know cereal and milk can be healthier. To me, a more likely scenario is the gradual emergence of a more benevolent, more pragmatic, and more efficient authoritarian leadership at the central as well as lower levels. And that's good enough—for China, for the larger Fourth Power, and for the world.

2

The Emergence of the Fourth Power

Most discussion of today's global economy centers on three powerhouses: North America, Europe, and Japan. In turn, economists usually divide Asia into Japan, a People's Republic of China that is rapidly changing and on the rise, and the industrialized "dragons" of South Korea, Taiwan, Hong Kong, and Singapore. Yet this standard economic definition doesn't match Pacific Rim realities. In Fact, Chinese businesses—many of which are located outside the People's Republic itself—make up the world's fourth economic power.

—John Kao, "The Worldwide Web of Chinese Business"[13]

As early as the 17th century, European travelers described the Chinese living in South-East Asia as being like Jews. The parallels are many: long exile from a mother country to which a deep cultural attachment nonetheless persists, apartness at best and genocide at worst in many of the adoptive countries, a strong commercial bent. The difference is the mother country. Israel matters only because it slots into the interests of greater forces. China is a giant that could dominate the 21st century.

—*The Economist*, "The Overseas Chinese"[14]

In his *The Borderless World* published in 1990,[15] economic strategist Kenichi Ohmae of Japan talked about the emergence of what he called the Interlinked Economy (ILE) of the Triad—the United States, Europe, and Japan, with participation by "aggressive economies such as Taiwan, Hong Kong, and Singapore." He said the ILE was becoming so powerful that it had swallowed most consumers and corporations of the world. Ohmae estimated the ILE's population to be about 1 billion with an average $10,000 per capita GNP. Most of the wealth in the world would be created, consumed, and redistributed in the ILE. Ohmae predicted that the ILE would, toward the twenty-first century, encompass most East European countries, most Asian newly industrialized economies (NIEs), and some Latin American countries. He sounded a little bit too romantic when he suggested that the policy objective for the ILE would be "ensuring the free flow of information, money, goods, and services as well as the free migration of people and corporations." But he was absolutely right to say no economy would be able to go too far if it was left out of the ILE.

Ohmae, being a strategist, seemed to have made a mistake in excluding China as a power that must be reckoned with. Apparently his formulation of the ILE was based on the integration of three economic powers, namely, the United States, European Community (now European Union), and Japan, which formed what he called the Triad. Ohmae's thinking was quite unstrategic when he decided, as late as 1990, not to reckon with an economy with a population of 1.2 billion and a nearly double-digit annual growth rate unbroken since 1979. The Triad was a mindset in which a powerful China did not belong. An economy bearing a non-capitalist label belongs elsewhere.

How these Chinese economies—the economy of the Chinese mainland, the economy of Taiwan, the economy of Hong Kong, and the economies of Chinese family businesses in other parts of the world should be politically or economically categorized—socialist or capitalist, planned or market or both—misses the point. What is important here is their increasing integration into a powerful economic reality. It is the emergence of the Fourth Power with the Chinese mainland as the driving force and other Chinese economies located on the periphery of the People's Republic as equally important business players. *The Fourth Power is not an economic alliance, nor is it a preconceived, carefully planned protectionist trade circle.*[16] *Still less is it a politically motivated conspiracy aimed at the Triad. This is a self-forming, highly flexible structure involving radically different political back-grounds. Its coming together has little to do with component political beliefs—they could be oceans apart politically.* Many suggest that the member economies are coming together because they are all Chinese and share the same culture. Others say that overseas Chinese come to invest in the main-land because they want to help. Still others, citing such examples as Chinese investors from Taiwan flocking to Fujian Province and Chinese from Hong Kong going to neigh-boring Guangdong Province to open factories, believe that the motive behind this "return" movement is to glorify their ancestors. Each of these cultural theories makes some sense, but leaves the larger picture unexplained. I believe that *the Chinese are coming together economically—not politically or ideologically—mainly because they are driven by a hard-to-resist economic logic and a shared cultural/business frame-work. The role that a shared heritage (speaking the same language, for example) plays in the process is as much instru-mental as cultural.* I will in the following pages identify certain trends to suggest that the emergence of the Fourth Power is real. As a formidable economic force, the Fourth Power will challenge as well as benefit the Triad in the near future and possibly well into the twenty-first century.

The Center Stage—Mainland China

There is little doubt that the center stage of the emerging Fourth Power is the mainland China. How and why China has become what it is today should be left for historians to ponder over. According to statistics compiled in 1993 by the United Nations, the annual worldwide GDP growth rate for the period 1971 to 1980 averaged 5.6 percent. When levels of development were accounted for, 3.4 percent was registered for developed economies; 5.4 percent for the former Soviet Union and East European countries; and 5.6 percent for developing countries. China, still beset by the Cultural Revolution in the first half of the recorded period, reaped a 5.9 percent rate of growth. A low initial baseline seemed to account for the relatively high growth rate for China, but it was nevertheless impressive given the fact that the Cultural Revolution (1966–76) had brought an extra burden to a Stalinistic planned economy.

China's economy gradually lifted itself up as of 1979 when Deng had started his economic reform.[17] During the period from 1981 through 1990, according to UN statistics, the world's annual GDP growth rate was an average 2.8 percent. The advanced economies averaged 2.8 percent, the former Soviet Union and Eastern Europe 2.2 percent, and developing nations 3.2 percent. China enjoyed a much higher GDP growth rate—a formidable 8.7 percent and became the fastest-growing economy in the world. It could be misleading and costly from the point of view of economic competition, if one continued to claim that China's baseline distorted the figures. By the end of 1990, China's GDP, if calculated on a Purchasing Power Parity basis, was in fact quite close to Japan's. Table 2.1 shows world GDP growth rates in the years 1990, 1991, and 1992.

Table 2.1. World Annual GDP Growth Rate Comparison

	1990	1991	1992
World average	1.7%	0.6%	0.6%
Developed Economies	2.4	0.7	1.5
Eastern Europe and former Soviet Union	5.0	-16.0	-14.7
Developing nations	3.4	3.4	4.0
China	5.2	7.0	12.8

The Chinese Academy of Social Sciences released in April 1993 the results of a research project it had completed in collaboration with two American universities in which it predicted that *China's GDP by the year 2020 will approach the same level as that of the United States in the same year. During a 30-year period between 1991 and 2020, China's economic growth will be among the world's fastest at an initial rate of around 8 percent and later leveling off at 7 percent. The average annual growth rate is expected to be 7.5 percent.* The development of the economy will be characterized by hypergrowth in transportation and telecommunications, a stable increase in agricultural production, and a balanced growth in light and heavy industries. China's savings rate will continue to rise, and rise rapidly, and it is predicted that starting from the year 2010 the country's increase in consumption will be faster than its increase in income. It is also predicted that the increase in investment over the three decades will be 11 percent, 8 percent, and 7.6 percent respectively. The main driving force, among other factors, lies in the great potential of international and domestic trade backed by a huge market both outside and inside China.

One of the most important trends in China's economic activities is that a considerable portion of China's GDP growth in recent years lies in its international trade. I see this as a healthy development considering China's long history of practicing a closed-door policy; it is now becoming increasingly integrated with the global economy. However, it also presents risks for the Chinese economy in that increasing interaction spells greater dependency on the "climate" of the world economy, and the Chinese economy will prosper or suffer in turn. But at this point the increasing participation of China's economy in the global system should be read as a good sign for the world as for China since China will be further encouraged to behave like a full member of the international community while its manufacturers and traders will be forced to remain committed to providing the market with value-added competitive products. These figures seem to me to be more compellingly suggestive than a dozen New York Times editorials and other liberal voices urging China to stay open and be a good boy: in the past decade or so whereas China's annual GDP growth averaged 9 percent, its annual increase in the total volume in imports and exports registered a high 13 percent. According to statistics based on the then prices and official exchange rates, China's dependency on international market was only 9 percent in 1978. Such dependency jumped to 39.5 percent in 1992. In comparison, such advanced economies as the United States, Japan, Germany, France, and Italy had an average 24.4 percent dependency rate in 1990. In the first eight months of 1993, China's total volume of imports and exports reached 77.84

billion dollars, representing, when based on official exchange rates, a 30 percent dependency of the nation's economy.

Economic indicators do not seem to suggest that China's high dependency on international market will soon come down. It has been estimated that imports during China's 1991–95 Eighth Five Year Plan could be between $300 billion and $350 billion. It seems reasonable to suggest that after China becomes a World Trade Organization member and continues to improve its foreign exchange control system, the dependency of its economy could reach as high as over 50 percent. Such a dependency is expected to fall with a steady GDP Growth and a rapid increase in the purchasing power of the *yuan*.[18]

Figures and numbers are abstract and do not convey a strong image. Sometimes people need to see, to feel, to be there. Few visitors to China did not return not impressed by the massive scale of capital construction projects going on in a vast expanse of yellow earth. The only advice I would like to give my friends who are traveling to China is for them to prepare for dirt on their shoes, dirt on their shirts and dresses, and dirt in their hair. Basically, tourists would travel through a world of dirt-filled construction sites. The development and growth has been too obvious for anyone to miss. Take a look at China's turn-of-the-century cradle of capitalism—Shenzhen.

Shenzhen, the Chinese city bordering Hong Kong, was the first Special Economic Zone (SEZ) designated by Deng Xiaoping. It received the official designation of city in 1980 when its population reached 300,000 (small by Chinese standards). Today, its population numbers 2.61 million, eight times more. Over a decade ago, there were only a few small agricultural machine-tool factories with a combined industrial output of no more than 70 million *yuan*. Today, boasting of as many as thirty industries including electronics and other high-tech enterprises, Shenzhen generates as much as thirty-seven billion *yuan* in industrial output. Its foreign trade has reached over 7 billion *yuan*, only second to Shanghai. Back in 1980, a few five-story buildings topped Shenzhen's downtown skyline in a area no larger than three square kilometers. Now, within an expanded area of 71 square kilometers, there have been constructed over one hundred high-rises, among which the highest is a 53-floor mammoth structure, Shenzhen's World Trade Center located in the Luohu District. Just within a short span of twelve years, a backward county seat which few Chinese had ever heard of has become one of China's most advanced cities.

Deng, taking credit for the growth the whole world has witnessed in Shengzhen, once said that it was his mistake not to include Shanghai in the first list of Special Economic Zones at the very beginning of the economic reform. But Shanghai is fast catching up with the backing of Beijing's Politburo, many of whose members once worked in positions such as mayor of Shanghai (Party Chief Jiang Zemin and Vice-Premier Zhu Rongji), or have strong ties with Shanghai, such as Qiao Shi, now President of the People's Congress. Shanghai is indeed becoming an important window through which one can see the pace of China's economic reform—particularly its reform in state enterprises—and observe the dynamics of the country's politics.

A Mass Sponge Metaphor

Before I discuss other players in the emerging Fourth Power, I would like to introduce what I call the mass sponge metaphor (please imagine natural sponges, not artificial ones). The European Union, the United States, and Japan are each a big sponge which has an enormous capacity to absorb investment, technology, labor, trade, infrastructure such as roads, highways, telecommunications, education, and all other standards by which to measure economic growth. Western Europe has absorbed across 500 years, the United States across 200 years—the rate of absorption accelerated after 1820 for both Europe and the United States—and Japan across 50 years registered a much faster rate of absorption. European business activities before the early sixteenth century were confined to the continent. Then the Portuguese, the Spanish, the Dutch, and the French sailed to South America, Africa, and Asia to establish colonialist posts and started "absorbing" abroad. Of course, the British later became the world's largest colonialist empire with their footprints left all over the globe. No other sponge had absorbed as much as the British until the United States came onto the stage. The twentieth century has first been the century of the United States, and then that of Japan, the two greatest sponges the world has ever seen. And they have absorbed at a much faster rate than Europeans did earlier. The Western European sponge, which has absorbed across hundreds of years, has become very full and worn. The American sponge is also very full and has shown signs of wear in some areas. The Japanese sponge is the first example to show the world that non-Western sponges can also absorb and may absorb even better. This is further proven in Taiwan, South Korea, Hong Kong, and Singapore, where truly better, high-capacity sponges have been found.

When a sponge is full of water, it stops absorbing. You have to press the water out before it is capable of absorbing again, or you let the water evaporate for it to gradually resume its absorptive capacity. Pressing the water out of a worn or even a partially aged sponge is dangerous because if you press too hard, the sponge will break and may permanently lose its ability to absorb. Letting the water evaporate takes time. Both the Western European sponge and American sponge are relatively full; the difference is that the former has been less dynamic than the latter since the end of World War II. The Japanese sponge is young, but is becoming full fast.

The Chinese sponge, a huge mass, is hungry for water. And water is plenty available while the conditions seem to favor high absorptive capacity. By the year 2020, as I indicated earlier, this mammoth sponge will have absorbed so much water that the total volume absorbed (in the form of GDP) will have equaled that of the American sponge. *To compare how much water a particular sponge has absorbed misses the point of this so-called sponge metaphor. The key point that I try to make is how much absorptive capacity remains in a particular sponge and how far it can possibly go until it reaches its physical limits.* Here lies the crucial difference between the Fourth Power and the other three powers. Again, to compare China and the United States, the size of the economy of the People's Republic and that of the United States will approximate each other by the year 2020, although the per-capita GDP of the former will remain at least five times less than that of the latter. For sure the Chinese economy will still be less developed and less sophisticated than its American counterpart, leaving much room for further expansion and improvement. This is to say, *by the year 2020 the Chinese economy will have become the world's largest or second largest single country economy and its annual growth rate will have slowed down to probably 4 or 5 percent or less. Still it will remain one of the most dynamic working sponges on earth.* And that is something that the other three powers cannot afford to overlook. Europe and the United States will find it more and more challenging to compete against China and the Fourth Power unless they quickly go high-tech, but China and the Fourth Power will go high-tech too, possibly soon after history rolls into the twenty-first century.

For the sponge metaphor to be practically meaningful, three basic conditions must be satisfied. First, you must have a large-size, densely textured sponge. If it is too small, it won't matter too much to the global economy. If its texture is not dense enough, its absoptive capacity is limited despite its size. In this regard, there are three big sponges that warrant the world's attention: China, Russia, and India. At the present time it seems that the Chinese sponge, large and favorably textured, is most ready to absorb and indeed is already absorbing feverishly. Second, you must have plenty of water for the sponge to absorb. Here I mean investment, availability of inexpensive but relatively skilled labor, the potential for infrastructure development, a lion's mouth for imports, mature but not necessarily sophisticated industries producing high-tech goods for export, a billion or half a billion hungry consumers, and other growth factors. If you, for example, have no money coming in, no money to save, no money to spend on consumer goods, and no vigorous import and export activities, you have no water. Luckily, the Chinese have water, lots of it. Third, you must have favorable conditions which facilitate the process of absorption. Here I refer to the existence of a common cultural/business framework.

Presumably there has existed a common framework within each of the existing economic powers, and there must also be one common to all. For the emerging Fourth Power, there exists a unique Chinese common cultural/business framework which has facilitated and will continue to facilitate business activities conducted by the Chinese on the mainland as well as those living on the periphery.

The so-called sponge metaphor is, after all, a metaphor. No metaphors are perfect or even make any sense beyond a narrowly defined context or point in time. People are finding it increasingly difficult to predict things beyond too long a period of time; the world is changing too fast and in too chaotic a way. But the basics remain solidly unchanged, and it seems that the players in the Fourth Power as well as in the existing powers will stick to the basics and be prepared for the unpredictable.

Key Players—The Diaspora

Undoubtedly the center stage of the Fourth Power is the Chinese mainland. However, the key engines, besides mainland Chinese, are rich, entrepreneurial Chinese living on the periphery, which I will label the Chinese Diaspora. As I explained earlier, for the convenience of categorization, I treat all Chinese physically living outside the mainland, including those in Taiwan, as belonging to the Chinese Diaspora (table 2.2).

The 55 million overseas Chinese, including those residing in Taiwan and Hong Kong, are a small number when compared with 1.2 billion living on the mainland. Why are they so important to the emergence of the Fourth Power? What power do they have? First, out of the four Asian "dragons" (the so-called newly industrialized economies or NIEs), two and three-quarters are Chinese. Taiwan is a Chinese dragon. Hong Kong is also a Chinese dragon. The Singapore dragon, too, looks more Chinese than anything else. Second, within four countries that belong to the Association of South East Asian Nations (ASEAN)—Indonesia, Thailand, Malaysia, and the Philippines—the Chinese, a minority in each of these countries, control an unbelievably large share of the respective

Table 2.2. The Chinese Diaspora (Ethnic Chinese in millions)

Taiwan	21.0
Hong Kong	6.0
Singapore	2.0
Indonesia	7.2
Thailand	5.8
Malaysia	5.2
Philippines	0.8
Burma	1.5
Vietnam	0.8
Rest of Asia and Australia	1.8
United States	1.8
Canada	0.6
Latin America	1.0
Europe	0.6
Africa	0.1

Source: Overseas Chinese Economy Yearbook.

economies. A study of Indonesia in the mid-1980s estimated that of assets owned by neither foreigners nor the government, 70–75 percent belonged to ethnic Chinese, who were only 4 percent of the Indonesian population. The Chinese controlled seventeen of the twenty-five biggest business groups. For example, the companies owned by the family of Liem Sioe Liong produced as much as 5 percent of Indonesia's GDP. An early study of Thailand showed that ethnic Chinese, who represented 8–10 percent of the total population, owned 90 percent of the country's commercial and manufacturing assets and half the capital of its banks. Ethnic Chinese account for one-third of the Malaysian population and yet control a much larger share of that country's economy. In the Philippines, ethnic Chinese, who represent less than one percent of the population, control two-thirds of the sales of the sixty-seven biggest commercial outfits. The Chinese are said to dominate the smaller businesses even more. To put into perspective the size of wealth of Asia's non-mainland Chinese, the 1990 GNP of Asia's 51 million overseas Chinese including those in Taiwan and Hong Kong was conservatively estimated at $450 billion—one-fourth larger than China's 1990 GNP,[19] calculated on a non-PPP basis. So which part is bigger, the 1.2 billion or the 55 million (including overseas Chinese residing outside of Asia)? It's hard to say. What is easy to say, however, is that when the two parts come together, it will be very big. And that is the Fourth Power.[20]

Coming Together

Mere size—1.2 billion consumers on the one side, or $450 billion GNP on the other—doesn't mean much. But when they come together—and they are coming together, and fast—that's something one must take seriously. While the governments are still trading insults, investors and traders are toasting their latest deals with *"ganbei"* ("bottoms up" in Chinese) and celebrating another contract they've just signed, using the same Chinese language, of course.

Eight years ago, I made a stop at Hong Kong's Kai Tak Airport on my way to Australia—the very first time I landed on the soil of Hong Kong. I had a strange feeling: I felt I had landed on an alien island far away, even though I knew China's Guangdong Province and Hong Kong had begun their economic relationship. In May 1993, I made my first trip to Hong Kong and I stayed at the Royal Park Hotel in Shatin. I couldn't believe I was in Hong Kong! I thought this must be Guangzhou or Shanghai or Beijing or any other Chinese city, but not Hong Kong: there were too many mainland Chinese wandering around, in the hotel lobby or on the streets, speaking Mandarin, or Shanghai dialect, or another Chinese dialect. Hong Kong is not yet part of the PRC; it will be returned legally to China on 30 June 1997. But they are very much interrelated already. I also know Taiwan and the mainland are fast coming together economically, though certainly not politically or ideologically. And I couldn't believe everything comes so fast. Just a few years ago, the mere thought of having a personal stake mingled with people from Taiwan could frighten me. I still remember vividly what happened during the 1966–76 Cultural Revolution: if you were found, for example, to have a relative living in Taiwan, your career would be finished overnight if you were lucky, or you went to jail. Now I can even travel to Taiwan if I want to. People who have not had the kinds of experiences that I and my fellow Chinese countrymen have had, may find my feelings and thoughts peculiar. Nevertheless, these were feelings and thoughts stained with tears and blood and lifelong remorse. Gradually these feelings and thoughts are being replaced by perceptions of an emerging scene: the Chinese are quietly coming together despite their political and ideological differences.

It has been reported that of all foreign direct investment in China up until the end of 1992, two-thirds came from Hong Kong and Taiwan. Four-fifths of all investment by Hong Kong has gone to Guangdong Province, where the same Cantonese dialect is spoken. Hong Kong investors and traders are now eyeing Shanghai, Beijing, Jiangsu, Zhejiang, Shandong, or wherever investment conditions are more attractive. While small- and medium-sized businesses from Taiwan continue to look for places to invest or partners with whom to form joint ventures in Fujian Province just across the Taiwan Strait, large companies are also on the move and are looking for opportunities elsewhere on the mainland.

Things are happening too fast for any author to be able to provide readers with updated information by the time his or her book appears on the shelves of bookstores. I would warn against readers treating numbers and figures too seriously. What is more important is the trend(s) behind the numbers and figures. At the time of drafting this chapter, a report was issued stating that China approved more than 44,000 new foreign-funded enterprises in the first eight months of 1993. Hong Kong, which invested in 27,687 firms in the same period, remains the largest source of foreign funds for enterprises in China. Taiwan comes the second with investment in 5,577 firms. The trend is that overseas Chinese money continues to flow to China in massive sums.[21]

It is only too natural for Hong Kong investors and business people to establish themselves on the mainland, knowing that the British colony will be returned to China on 30 June 1997. Mainland Chinese know what Hong Kong is and how Hong Kong can help to boost China's international trade, offering a high stake in China's GDP growth far beyond the next decade. Again figures are not as informative as the trend behind the figures. It has been reported that by having pumped somewhere around U.S. $12 billion into the Hong Kong economy by the end of 1992, China has become the biggest source of direct foreign investment in the territory. Japan by the end of its fiscal year in March 1993 followed with a total of $11.5 billion. The investment from United States was estimated at $8.5 billion by the end of 1992. A Hang Seng Bank report says Chinese interests have bought into Hong Kong for the same reason investors from other countries have found the territory attractive. They have found Hong Kong's infrastructure and noninterventionist policy conducive to the conduct of international trade and investment, which help raise the foreign exchange earnings of the country. The Hang Seng report also says investors from China have been among the most active groups of overseas investors in the territory in recent years. Apart from the large and prominent companies which have a long operating tradition in Hong Kong, a multitude of mainland interests, including those run by provinces and municipalities, have also established a presence in the territory.

Obviously *China's proximity, resources, market potential, skilled but inexpensive labor, world-class scientists in select fields, and huge pool of talent, to cite just a few factors, are what have attracted Hong Kong's low-, mid-, and now high-tech industries. From the Chinese mainland's perspective, Hong Kong's strategic position as one of the world's most important financial and trade centers, its capital, management experience, market knowledge, and worldwide business connections will become some of the most precious resources that China can possibly locate anywhere in the world.*

Yet something seems missing. When mainland Chinese—officials or nonofficials—talk about Hong Kong, they talk about its wealth, its Cantonese dialect (which most Chinese don't speak or understand), its high-rises, its shopping, its restaurants, its laissez-faire business philosophy, and its beautiful oceanic scenery. They all miss one thing: its rule of law and relative absence of corruption, which is quite different from Taiwan and the mainland. To me, this is something far more important to the mainland where man is still larger than law and corruption is an ingredient of business and social life. I think mainland Chinese could benefit immensely by emulating their compatriots in Hong Kong in their practice of law. But I have a practical concern: now that dealing with mainland Chinese has become part of their daily life, "How can you not wet your shoes when you often walk along a river?" as the popular Chinese saying goes. I think it would be to the benefit of both the territory and its giant motherland that efforts be made by both sides to maintain Hong Kong's relatively clean business dealings after the integration of the two economies has become more institutionalized.

Taiwan has been ambivalent toward the mainland in recent years. How can you not be when the memory of the past is still lingering in your mind? But things are fast changing. On 2 November 1987, Chiang Ching-kuo lifted the thirty-eight-year-old absolute ban on visits to the mainland. In August 1988 the permission was authorized to trade with the mainland via a third country or area. In April 1989, two months before the Tiananmen Square tragedy, journalists were allowed to make reporting trips to the mainland. From June 1990 on, Taiwan permitted visits by mainland scholars, artists and athletes. Then on 1 May 1992, President Lee declared an end to the "Period of National Mobilization for Suppressing Communist Rebellion." On paper, there are still "Three No's": no contact; no negotiation; no compromise. In reality, there have been numerous contacts, numerous negotiations, and numerous compromises. Since the ban on visiting the mainland was lifted late in 1987, millions of Taiwanese have traveled to the mainland. The total value of Taiwan's indirect trade with the mainland through Hong Kong approached $7 billion in 1992, a substantial increase over the $5.8 billion invested in 1991 and double the $3.5 billion invested in 1990.

How can the mainland not be attractive to Taiwanese businessmen? Labor is a tenth of the price in Taiwan. Land is a hundredth or even a thousandth of the price on the island. Plus a market with 1.2 billion potential consumers!

The economic integration of Taiwan and the mainland is simply irresistible. And they are coming together despite all the political roadblocks.

Taiwan, as is known to all, is one of Asia's four economic dragons. Even though past experiences cannot chart an economy's future, they can always be used as a mirror. Taiwan's miracle has already been included in the textbook for mainland China's economic planners and managers to study. Taiwan's development strategies could be more complicated than suspected. But even people who have little knowledge of basic economics can understand why Taiwan has walked the road it has walked. Taiwan's development strategy for the 1950s was designed to save precious foreign exchange by reducing its need for imports. It therefore developed its own canning and food-processing industries, textiles, its own cement, plywood, and glass factories. In 1960, the Statute for the Encouragement of Investment was passed, under which the government gave preferential interest rates for time deposits, soaking up the savings of the society, and then lent the money at subsidized rates to launch labor-intensive exporting industries. In 1966, the year when the Cultural Revolution was undertaken on the mainland, Taiwan's first export-processing zone was set up to attract foreign investment and boost exports, and it soon became very successful. By the end of the 1960s, Taiwan had become a major rival to Hong Kong, selling to the world such labor- or capital-intensive goods as clothing, sewing machines, radios, televisions, synthetic fibers, and fertilizers, which earned Taiwan substantial foreign exchange. The 1970s saw the establishment of heavy industries on the island such as iron and steel and basic petrochemicals to supply Taiwan's manufacturers of autos, ships, toys, machinery, and electrical consumer goods. The 1980s saw Taiwan go "upmarket" with the development of its personal computer industry and other high-tech areas. The 1990s will be marked by ten so-called newly emerging industries: telecommunications; information; consumer electronics; semiconductors; precision machinery and automation; aerospace; advanced materials; specialty chemicals and pharmaceuticals; medical and health care; and pollution control. It makes sense for Taiwan to move "upmarket" where brain power and capital matter more than labor costs. Taiwan can no longer compete against its cheaper competitors in making such labor-intensive goods as shoes, umbrellas, handbags, and toys since wage rates are fast rising, land is becoming more expensive, and environmental controls are becoming stricter relative to the mainland across the strait.

Definitely, Taiwan can move low- or mid-tech industries to the mainland where both labor and land are much cheaper and environmental controls are less strict. This is exactly what has been happening. But what about the ten emerging industries which are all high-tech? These industries need enormous amounts of capital and state of the art scientific capacity. The problem with Taiwan is that it has neither the equivalents of South Korean *chaebol* (conglomerates) nor anything like Japan's giant trading companies. It instead has 700,000 small or medium-sized businesses. Will Taiwan go to the mainland to shop for world-class scientists and big joint venture opportunities in order to jointly move "upmarket?" If it does, it will be a blessing for the Fourth Power.[22]

Hong Kong and Taiwan are two of the four Asian economic dragons, and their contribution to the emergence of the Fourth Power will be crucially important. But what about overseas Chinese in other Southeast Asian countries? Are they also joining in the race of "go back home?" As a matter of fact, many ASEAN Chinese businessmen are not only going home, but are making the Chinese mainland the focus of their corporate growth for the next decade. And their investment strategies have characteristics which mark them out from earlier waves of Chinese investment originating in Hong Kong and Taiwan. Five distinguishing factors have been reported in *The Asian Business* to characterize the ASEAN Chinese investment strategies:[23]

1. They are motivated more by China's latent consumer demand than by its cheap labor costs and easy land acquisitions, which are already available to them in Southeast Asia. This means they are thinking far into the future.

2. They are helping to modernize China's primary indus-
    tries and build up its infrastructure with less interest in
    donating money to build hospitals and universities as a
    way of demonstrating goodwill. The message is that they
    are hard-core businessmen.
3. They are bringing to China the management skills they
    have successfully used in ASEAN to apply sophisticated
    Western technology in an underdeveloped environment.
    This suggests that they may understand the Chinese
    environment even better than their counterparts from
    Hong Kong and Taiwan.
4. They are advancing into places often ignored by other
    foreign investors since they have origins in a wide vari-
    ety of towns and provinces in China. This would help
    widen China's investment frontier and ease the tension
    that arises from an enlarged gap between China's more
    developed coastal areas and its underdeveloped inner
    provinces.
5. They are committing long-term investment to China, rather
    than seeking the quick profits to be generated from export
    processing. This is quite different from a certain number of
    investors from Hong Kong and Taiwan who are more
    opportunistic and more interested in making quick money.

Also in its April 1993 issue, *The Asian Business*[24]
reported a survey of recent major deals involving ASEAN
Chinese investors that total a massive $7.3 billion spread
over twelve projects covering Zhejiang, Fujian, Guangdong,
Yunnan, Beijing, Shanghai, and many other places. I agree
with the assessment of *The Asian Business* report that the
overseas Chinese in ASEAN and East Asia have spearheaded
almost every important business trend in Asia. By injecting
their unique style of capitalism into China, they will become
true Asian multinationals, and their stature in global markets will be even more formidable. There is little doubt that
ASEAN Chinese businessmen will be key players in the
formation of the Fourth Power.

To what extent will the Chinese economies—the mainland, Hong Kong, Taiwan, and ASEAN Chinese businesses—

be more dependent on each other than on the other three economic powers, namely Japan, the United States, and the European Union, is hard to determine as new patterns are unfolding around the world. One thing sure to happen is that they will become more closely integrated, and each will benefit from the other at a time when protectionism is on the rise in the Triad. Ohmae's notion of Interlinked Economy is certainly profound, and the Fourth Power won't be a power without being, strategically, a part of it. However, *the world is not yet borderless, either economically or politically. While the romanticism of borderlessness remains alluring, the reality of consolidating a single-market Europe and an enlarged NAFTA may speed up the process of the formation of the Fourth Power even though this will by no means be a protectionist move on the Chinese part.*

3

Common Cultural/Business Framework: The Key to Understanding Doing Business in China

Traditional Chinese culture is . . . widely considered to be built upon a value system crystallized in Confucianism. Confucianism itself has shown its "elasticity" through interpretations over the past two thousand years. All schools of Confucianism agree, however, that this traditional value system is revealed through elaborate definitions, regulations, and moral and ethical principles regarding individuals' roles and relationships. These principles are not just ideas; they are materialized in social practices, including rituals, rites, ceremonies, and cultural artifacts.

—Pan, Chaffee, Chu, and Ju, *To See Ourselves*[25]

It does not reveal the whole picture to say that overseas Chinese flock to China to invest or conduct other kinds of business because that is where the fastest-growing economy is. It is equally insufficient to reason that rich Chinese from Hong Kong go to Guangdong Province to invest and Taiwanese Chinese arrive in Fujian Province to launch joint ventures because that is where their ancestors came from. I believe *the main rationale behind the integration of the Chinese economies is that they share a common cultural/business framework which makes doing business easier as well as more culturally and psychologically gratifying. Uniquely Chinese, this framework is unwritten and unspoken, but is tacitly understood and shared among those who conduct business together.* It is cultural in nature and can be defined by what I call pragmatic-humanistic rationalism which has a deep root in Confucianism. Before I describe the key components of this framework, I will first explain what I mean by pragmatic-humanistic rationalism.

Pragmatic-Humanistic Rationalism

Because of the omnipresence of Confucianism in traditional Chinese culture which moralizes and politicizes every aspect of the Chinese way of life, Chinese society has all along for the past two thousand years been very mundane, very political, and very pragmatic. Chinese philosophy, for example, never quite gained an ontological status that went beyond moral and political confines. In other words, Chinese philosophy is more of a philosophy of moralities than a philosophy in its pure sense; it is always related to "this life in this world." Religion, as a belief system or as a way of life, was never quite able to define the "Chineseness" of the Chinese people. It is Confucianism that does the job. It is not difficult to understand why a nonreligious people tend to be more pragmatic than idealistic.

Chinese science is another good example by which to explain why traditional Chinese mode of thinking is pragmatic-rationalistic in nature. In traditional China, science was never developed for the sake of developing science; science, like philosophy, was very much politicized. And more often than not people equated science with technology which, of course, could be used to solve practical problems of "this life in this world." Deng Xiaoping's "cat theory" is a modern version of pragmatic rationalism. He says: "It doesn't matter whether it's a black cat or white cat; it's a good cat as long as it catches mice." Indeed, this "cat theory" has been attractive for mainland Chinese who for three decades were subjected to a Maoist utopian mode of thinking which threw the whole nation into confusion. The Chinese can never quite live comfortably without practicing pragmatic rationalism (I guess that's another reason why Maoism was destined to come to grief as a utopian ideology). Deng's "cat theory" was also widely acclaimed by overseas Chinese in Taiwan, Hong Kong, or elsewhere in the world as that which would save China, and not without good reason. It is pragmatic rationalism that has served as the basis on which Chinese—mainlanders and overseas Chinese—started to build mutual trust and confidence again.

Pragmatic rationalism is only one side of the coin. The other side is Chinese humanism, or humanistic rationalism. Chinese humanism is not to be confused with Western humanism. Western humanism sees man as a social animal, an independent entity with reason, emotion, volition, love, friendship, equality, dignity, human rights, who is responsible for his own destiny. Western humanism, a revolt against the Church and feudalism in the Middle Ages, gave full play to man's individuality. In contrast, Chinese humanism went the other way. It is aimed at perfection of the moral self (*xiushen*) to its most practical objectives: regulation of family relationships (*qijia*); good government of state (*zhiguo*); and peace under heaven (*pingtianxia*). Without these objectives, man is morally and ethically deficient and inhumane. A man who knows how to suppress individuality in accordance with *xiushen qijia zhiguo pingtianxia* is a moral man, an ethical man, even a noble man. Man can learn to suppress his individuality through *kejifuli* (control self and restore rites), according to Confucius. The key word is *li*, which can be said to represent the very core of Confucianism. Let me elaborate a bit on this concept, as this is the key to understanding not only Chinese humanism, but the common cultural/business framework which I will discuss later in this chapter.

The *li* that Confucius (551 B.C.E. – 479 B.C.E.) wanted to restore during his Spring and Autumn (Chungqiu) historical period originated from the rites of the Xia dynasty (c. 2,200 – c. 1,700 B.C.E.), the Shang dynasty (c. 1,700 – c. 1,100 B.C.E.), and the Zhou dynasty (c. 1,100 – 256 B.C.E.), the so-called "Three Dynasties" in Chinese history. Confucius did not create any rites by himself; his efforts were aimed at reviving the ethics and rites of the "Three Dynasties." *Li* as a set of rites and proprieties governing social norms and institutions underwent all kinds of changes throughout the Chinese history, but its essence continued to lie in the strict distinction of social ranks and strata. Preeminent among them was the so-called "Three Cardinal Principles," or *sangang*, which include *jun wei chen gang*, or "Ruler guides subject"; *fu wei zi gang*, or "Father guides son"; and *fu wei qi gang*, or "Husband guides wife". The "Three Cardinal Principles" guided the practice of Chinese humanism in the past two thousand years. A subject was a good and humane person if he did what the emperor told him to do. A son was a good and humane son if he did what his father told him to do. And a wife was a good and humane wife if she did what her husband told her to do. Things have changed greatly in the past few decades: no more emperor; no more absolutely unchallengeable parental authority; and more and more women who have become less submissive and more assertive. Despite these changes, however, a good person is still very much defined by whether s/he knows his/her place and works hard to help maintain the existing social order, a new kind of humanistic rationalism, if you will.

Chinese humanistic rationalism, in modern business activities and practices, serves to regulate human relationships and inject order into a seemingly chaotic business world. Chinese humanistic rationalism holds serious implications for such important issues as organizational leadership succession, decision-making, management-labor relations, superior-subordinate relations, promotions, corporate culture, teamwork, and so on. In other words, Chinese humanistic rationalism determines how precious business resources are regulated. While pragmatic rationalism has always been followed among overseas Chinese businesses and began its comeback on the mainland toward the end of 1978 and early 1979 when Deng Xiaoping launched his economic reforms, humanistic rationalism is fast becoming a common frame of reference for both overseas Chinese and mainlanders who have very much shaken off the yoke of Maoist idealism and its legacy of class struggle.

Pragmatic-humanistic rationalism, as the cultural underpinnings of the common cultural/business framework, is expressed in various forms through a set of culturally and socially meaningful practices. I will now discuss its key components.

Key Components of Common Cultural/Business Framework

The notion of a common cultural/business framework as a set of unwritten or unspoken norms and proprieties which help to conduct business in a socially meaningful and mutually understandable way, is widely accepted and indeed well followed in business activities, whether such activities are regional, national, international, or transcultural. But how to define it and at what level to address it could be controversial since there are potentially so many dimensions involved. Here I are not talking about common cultural/business framework in the general sense. I will focus on the common cultural/business framework of the Chinese, with pragmatic-humanistic rationalism forming the cultural underpinnings of this framework. From a social/business resources perspective, *I see this unique Chinese common cultural/business framework as composed of two main aspects: what constitutes social/business resources and how they are regulated. Pragmatic rationalism seems to determine what comprises social/business resources, whereas humanistic rationalism tends to affect how such social/business resources are regulated.* Foremost among numerous social/business resources are *guanxi* or connections (as external resource) and entrepreneurial spirit (as internal resource). How such resources are regulated pertains to social hierarchy and role communication.

Guanxi and Entrepreneurial Spirit as
Social/Business Resources

Guanxi. *No one can claim he or she understands China if one does not know the two-character term* guanxi. *China is a land of* guanxi. *Chinese are a people living in* guanxi. *Nothing can be done without* guanxi. Guanxi *is a web of an individual person's blood and/or social connections which define who s/he is and what s/he is capable of accomplishing without accounting for other resources s/he has available for use.* I don't have any doubt that *guanxi*, thus defined, is the most important social/business resource of an individual Chinese. To say Mr. so and so has a lot of *guanxi* is to say he is a man of great social/business resources, a man one is not supposed to neglect. A person who doesn't have any *guanxi* is one who is socially isolated and probably can't go far beyond his or her social space. It is not just that *guanxi* makes things easier; it is that *guanxi* makes things happen. Even though the practice of *guanxi* among the Chinese may surpass the limit allowed by social ethics or law, it is nevertheless not necessarily unethical or illegal. Here I refer to not just mainland Chinese (though the mainland Chinese indisputedly lead in the practice of *guanxi* in Greater China), but the Chinese in Hong Kong or Taiwan or elsewhere in the world as well. When everybody—elite, commoners, as well as all organizations—practices *guanxi*, it has become a social institution, whether you like it or not. And social cybernetics will make sure that its practice, once out of balance, return it to normalcy.

While *guanxi* is practiced in all cultures and societies, it's a way of life in China and among Chinese communities. Theories have been developed to explain why *guanxi* has become part of the Chineseness in contemporary China and in Chinese communities everywhere. One theory attributes it to the rule of man being larger than the rule of law. This makes perfect sense considering the fact that throughout China's long history, and particularly during the four decades after the founding of the People's Republic, the emperor was the law, Mao was the law, and then in Taiwan Chiang Kai-shek and his Kuomintang were the law. When you had a case to present, for example, you didn't go to a court; you went to a government official knowing he was the law or above the law if there had ever been such a law.

Another theory says that the practice of *guanxi* was engendered by a scarcity of resources: when you can't get what you want through normal channels because too many people are waiting in line for too small a bag of rice, you try to get your *guanxi* to help. Still another theory postulates that practicing *guanxi* is simply practicing pragmatic rationalism; to be a Chinese, you don't go against what defines Chineseness. There is also a theory which hinges on Confucianism. A related concept is *renqing*, or "personal obligations and affections." It was the feeling of *renqing* that bound together many of the basically reciprocal social relations in traditional China. A practical manifestation of *renqing* is the asking and giving of a favor. In many instances, practicing *guanxi* is practicing *renqing*, and this happens among all Chinese.

What seems to be more important to me is less why *guanxi* is practiced than what it is and how it is practiced. First, all Chinese know *guanxi* as a social/business resource is important and thus must be practiced in due course, even though one doesn't have to acknowledge it publicly. The understanding is tacitly shared. Many Westerners are fast learning it. It's amazing that *guanxi* seems to be becoming the Chinese word most correctly pronounced by some Westerners and the sound has become so communicative between Chinese and their Western counterparts that a mere utterance of the sound *guanxi* is taken as the clearest indication that the nature of a particular business deal has been understood. The importance of *guanxi*, as many Westerners and their Chinese counterparts understand it, often lies not so much in how much honor one can get as in how practically useful the perceived *guanxi* could be or as in how routinely it is practiced as a cultural ritual.

Second, an effective way to understand Chinese *guanxi* is to understand it as a system, which requires one to develop a taxonomy. This introduces the concept of *guanxi-wang*, or a network of *guanxi*, which usually consists of two broad categories, blood *guanxi* and social *guanxi*. To understand one's *guanxi* is to understand one's *guanxiwang*—the network of one's blood *guanxi* and social *guanxi*—which can be so complicated that an outsider may never quite understand how it works. Blood *guanxi* may include one's family members, relatives, and members from the same clan. Social *guanxi* are all those connections which do not belong to one's blood *guanxi*, such as friends, colleagues, or ex-classmates. For an individual Chinese, it's extremely important to have some blood *guanxi* available for use in various situations. No matter how important one's social *guanxi* are, they can seldom reach the level of unquestionable trust that one's blood *guanxi* can enjoy. Godwin Chu, a senior researcher at the East-West Center of Hawaii, and I studied the recent cultural changes in China, in which we found that people's relations with relatives were closer than with friends and other social relations. Our study has found that blood *guanxi* may not necessarily be as significant as social *guanxi* in terms of their pragmatic "usefulness," but you can rely on the former most. When you are new in a particular field and uncertain about what is going to happen once you are in, you will definitely begin with your blood *guanxi* if you have any. For example, if I want to start a business in China and I have my brother and other important relatives living in Shanghai, I would probably start by talking it over with them before approaching any social *guanxi*, no matter how socially important members of the latter group are. And I would willingly put my resources in the hands of my brother or another trusted relative. You feel safe this way.

What about a Western businessman who has neither blood *guanxi* nor social *guanxi* in China? How can he get into the business game in China? Many different ways. Go in directly. Or find a middleman in Hong Kong. Or call the official who once visited with you and left a business card. Or, assuming your best friend is a Chinese immigrant living in the United States who has relatives living and working in China, just talk it over with your best friend and let him talk it over with his relatives back home in China. This may be a better way to start a business in China. This may sound highly improbable to the Westerne reader, but it happens.

I've been discussing the difference of blood *guanxi* versus social *guanxi* at the level of who to trust more in a general sense. I do not imply, however, that one cannot trust one's social *guanxi* and should not start things from there. One's social *guanxi*, or rather, social *guanxiwang* (network of social *guanxi*) is no less important than one's blood *guanxi*. As a matter of fact, one's social *guanxiwang* tends to be larger and cover a larger social space than one's blood *guanxiwang*. Indeed, an individual's social *guanxiwang*, if used skillfully, can be used with a freer hand since blood *guanxi* more easily fall victim to criticism of practicing favoritism. In real practice, one tends to pay more attention to and spend more energy on developing one's social *guanxiwang*; one doesn't have to worry too much about one's blood *guanxi*—they are always there and can be mobilized anytime one wants. One's social *guanxiwang* tends to follow a separate taxonomy such as primary versus secondary, long-term versus short-term, close versus casual, and so on. It is important to remember that one's social *guanxiwang* tends to be multitiered, following a hierarchy of systems and subsystems. For example, your ex-classmate, who has his or her own social *guanxiwang*, may be willing to share a portion of it with you, and as time goes on, those newly "enlisted," or rather, "given," members may gradually become your permanent resources.

Third, the Chinese *guanxi* system is reciprocal in nature. Nothing is worse than practicing *guanxi* as if following one-way traffic, a practice which is "unethical" in the eyes of many Chinese. A person who only gets from and never gives back to *guanxi* is an unethical person, someone one should avoid or stop doing business with. Each time you get something from *guanxi*, you know you're in debt in terms of *renqing*. And when you have performed a positive role in another's practice of *guanxi*, you would wait and see how the person treats you the next time you need his or her help. In other words, you will be sensitive to the reciprocity of *guanxi*. If, for any reason, you repeatedly fail to get what you had asked from a person who had enlisted you as part of his *guanxiwang*, you might decide that you have lost face and you might want to stop doing business with this person, letting him or her know, more often than not, through indirect communication. Many Westerners never quite learn the reciprocal nature of *guanxi* even when they consider themselves ace players in the Chinese game of *guanxi*. It's never enough to say "thank you, my friend, that's very kind of you to have done all this for me"; you must consciously realize you are in debt in terms of *renqing*, and remember you may have to pay it back one way or another or you risk losing this *guanxi* of yours who could be very important in your future business. It's not necessarily a one-for-one mechanical tally—it's seldom that way, as a matter of fact—but it should be reciprocal on the whole. Chinese tend to resent the tendency in which one quickly pays off the debt, so to speak, and terminates *guanxi* when the deal is done. One-shot practice of *guanxi* suggests low taste and opportunism.

Fourth, *guanxi* as an individual's social/business resource should be viewed more as a way of life and practiced as such. Western misunderstanding and, in some cases, resentment of the Chinese practice of *guanxi* is well understood, but it is also culturally biased. It is important for Westerners as well as many of their Chinese counterparts to correct their perception of *guanxi* and accept the practice of it as a routine cultural ritual in Chinese society. *In many situations, people practice* guanxi *not because they want to get anything done, but simply because they want to demonstrate their allegiance to and appreciation of their* guanxi *or simply because they want to assert their Chineseness in that practicing* guanxi *makes them an active part of the social fabric, or simply because it's a matter of ritualism. In other words, practicing* guanxi *is giving structure and order to social/business life, even though* guanxi *itself has no formal structure.* Few Westerners, and indeed not many Chinese, think that way. Too often people associate the practice of *guanxi* with Asian types of corruption. To me, with or without the practice of *guanxi*, Chinese are neither more nor less corrupt. This being said, I am not suggesting that *guanxi* or the practice of it is always good and clean. *guanxi*, unethically practiced—which could well be the case with anybody anywhere—descends to the level of favoritism and back-door dealings, which is common not only in the Chinese mainland, but among Chinese communities elsewhere in the world. But it doesn't have to be that way. *Guanxi* can be clean and can be practiced in a clean way.

If I have to choose one Chinese term to describe what I call the common cultural/business framework of the Chinese, I would not hesitate to say *guanxi*. To me, it's not only the greatest social/business resource an individual Chinese can hope to have, but the most important defining characteristic of the Chinese common cultural/business framework. Other components tend to be at the mercy of *guanxi*, including even entrepreneurial spirit in certain situations.

Entrepreneurial Spirit. If *guanxi* is defined as a person's external social/business resource, entrepreneurial spirit is his or her internal source of power. An entrepreneur, as is understood in the West, is someone who runs a business at his own financial risk. But the Chinese basically are not adventurers; they are culturally too sophisticated to be adventurers. Entrepreneurial spirit, in the Chinese interpretation, is a person's great urge to succeed at whatever cost. This may not be adventuristic. Rather, the entrepreneur is willing to do what is necessary to be ready for challenge. Look at the overseas Chinese. They started from practically nothing. They worked hard, twenty hours a day if necessary. They saved every penny they earned. They then put their life's savings into their children's education. Then they had their business, maybe a small family business. They succeeded. Were they not entrepreneurs? When they started, they had nothing to risk because they had practically nothing. After they were in, no matter how hard the conditions, they would hang on until they succeeded. They knew they were not working for their personal success. They were building their small empire, brick by brick, for their family, their ancestors. If you go to Hong Kong, Indonesia, Malaysia, Thailand, anywhere in the world where there are successful ethnic Chinese, you will hear the same story over and over again. Ask Chinese billionaire Li Ka-shing how he succeeded in building his multibillion-dollar empire in Hong Kong, which has been expanded to include ventures in mainland China, Canada, the United States, and other parts of the world. Ask millions of Chinese small family businesses. And ask some of today's newly wealthy in China. Are they not entrepreneurs? We are indeed talking about a special kind of entrepreneurial spirit. It is one with a Confucian imprint. It is one which, like *guanxi*, defines, at least partly, the Chineseness of the Chinese.

The Chinese entrepreneurial spirit on the mainland had long been suppressed until recently. In the late 1950s and early 1960s, China's "Great Leap Forward" movement launched by Mao and the three-year manmade natural disasters that followed the movement, sent millions of Chinese to death due to starvation. China was plunged into an utter chaos of lawlessness and disorder where millions upon millions of Chinese intellectuals and other "undesirable elements" were singled out for physical and spiritual humiliation in ways unheard of in history. Nobody knows how many people died. Nobody can possibly measure the loss China as a nation suffered in the 1966–76 Cultural Revolution. I am sure of one thing, however. That is, the entrepreneurial spirit of the Chinese remained strong, even though very much distorted thanks to the long years of the socialist practice of the "iron rice bowl" guaranteed from cradle to grave. As soon as Deng Xiaoping launched the economic reforms in 1979 and later put forward his "cat theory," the long-suppressed entrepreneurial spirit among the mainland Chinese began to gradually bloom again. The figures I reported in chapter 2 should sufficiently attest to the magic that the entrepreneurial spirit can create. Mainland China just represents a belated experience of practicing entrepreneurial spirit. Thanks to the same entrepreneurial spirit, economic magic occurred earlier in Hong Kong and Taiwan, and with other Chinese businesses in other parts of East Asia as part of the overall East Asian boom that began in the early 1960s. The practicing of entrepreneurial spirit has been a typical Chinese refusal to remain in poverty and insignificance as they saw others prosper. Taiwan's GDP per capita around 1960 was only $600. The mainland's GDP per head in 1962 toward the end of the three-year human-created natural disasters was a miserable $60, the world's eleventh-lowest. *The Economist* reported that, with almost a ten-year delay after Japan's economic recovery was officially recorded, the four dragons, namely Taiwan, Hong Kong, Singapore, and South Korea—over half of them being Chinese—impressed the world with their rise from poverty with real GDPs doubling every eight years during 1960–85 (around eightfold in all).[26] This mammoth growth was achieved mainly through their export-led industrial development. These Chinese economies realized over thirty years ago that their growth potential lay in trade. They all jumped on this, and they succeeded.

The Chinese entrepreneurial spirit, unlike the entrepreneurial spirit in the West, which is largely defined by a person's willingness to take risks, is characterized by three elements: the willingness to work hard, and sometimes under extremely hard conditions; the willingness to save as much as possible; and the willingness to do whatever it takes to invest in education.

First, the Chinese are among the world's hardest-working people when they know their efforts will be rewarded, even minimally. I don't have to go too far to look for evidence to prove it. The above-mentioned study Godwin Chu of the East-West Center of Hawaii and I did revealed some interesting data in this regard. We asked an open question: "What do you think is the most important element for career success?" Respondents were allowed to answer the question in whichever way they liked. Based on 1,424 respondents from China, nearly half of them mentioned "diligence," a strong indication that the traditional Chinese value of diligence (and frugality) as a way of life remained despite the disastrous ten-year Cultural Revolution. We asked another question related to a person's work ethic: "Which is more important to you, to treasure your time and work as hard as possible, or to enjoy while you can?" Nearly nine out of ten respondents (89.7 percent) said "treasure your time and work as hard as possible." We also asked some other questions related to this theme: "What kind of person do you prefer as your workmate, someone with a high ability even though not a close friend, or a close friend who does not have a high ability?" Not to our surprise, an overwhelming 92 percent of our respondents would like his or her workmate to be one with outstanding work ability even though not a close friend. We also asked: "If you were to pick a co-worker, which one would you prefer, someone who works very hard, but has no sense of humor, or someone who does a minimum of work, but is a lot of fun?" About four out of five of the Chinese sample would like to have one who works hard; having fun or no fun doesn't matter.

Second, entrepreneurial spirit is mere talk if one does not have a means of coming up with needed capital with which to invest. The Chinese and their other East Asian neighbors as well are very good at accumulating capital by, among other means, saving. The Chinese are among the world's greatest savers, which has been another important success factor for their economies in the past thirty years. By the 1990s East Asia (excluding Japan), with the Chinese economies and businesses as its backbone, was saving more than 36 percent of GDP, unmatched in any of the rest of the world's economies, developed or developing. And they have been investing almost as much as they save. China's savings rate has been between 33 and 35 percent. I heard a story which tells how a Chinese farmer saves: each time the farmer has accumulated 51 cents, he would borrow 49 cents from whomever he can borrow to make it one dollar, and deposit it in his bank account. He then forces himself to work hard to earn 49 cents to pay back the debt since he can't stand the idea of being in debt. His urge to save is so strong that he borrows to save! Saving has become the farmer's way of life and he enjoys it more than anything else.

Third, when you have money plus a pair of diligent hands, you are not yet entrepreneurial in the unique Chinese sense. You are not yet entrepreneurial because you cannot go far. To achieve big success, you need a smarter head. You need ideas. You need knowledge. You need to understand modern technologies. Confucius says: "One who works with his mind (knowledge) rules; one who works with his hands is ruled." Whether you like it or not, this is still very much the reality of the world we live in. A traditional Chinese saying goes: "In books there are houses piled with gold." The Chinese—here I am referring to Chinese individuals, not the government—understand that education holds the key to a person's career success. You yourself might not be lucky enough to have parents who could afford to send you to school, but you don't want to see the same thing happen to your children. Most Chinese pin their hopes on their children, who are expected to become "as glorious as dragons," as a popular Chinese saying goes.

In traditional China, the only path for upward mobility was education. If one passed the state examinations, one could enter the world of imperial service. The value of education, except during certain historical periods like the Cultural Revolution in the mainland, has all along been highly upheld. Most Chinese parents are willing to save every penny to ensure that their children have a good education. In our previously mentioned study of the Chinese, we asked our subjects a key question: "What do you want most in life?" We gave fourteen possible goals for them to choose from. Quite to our expectation, "successful children" received the second highest endorsement (66.2 percent) after "warm and close family," the number one choice (79.8 percent). We also asked two similar questions: "If you have a son, how far will you support him in school? If you have a daughter, how far will you support her in school?" The results for sons and daughters were nearly identical. More than 80 percent of the Chinese are willing to support their sons and daughters through either college or graduate school. Keep in mind that in China, only a very small percentage of high school graduates have the privilege of attending college due to the enormous size of the population and limited availability of educational resources.

The notion of Chinese entrepreneurial spirit, which consists of a person's willingness to work hard, willingness to save to accumulate capital, and willingness to invest in education, as an internal social/business resource is widely shared among mainland and overseas Chinese alike even though they have been living in quite different social and political systems. Most Chinese believe that *when one has what I call the "Four Treasures": a pair of diligent hands, capital, a good education, and* guanxi, *one can be said to have arrived at the starting line of his or her success. To make it to the finish line, however, one needs to do more.* This leads me to the other side of the means of regulating social/business resources, the second half of the Chinese common cultural/business framework.

The Importance of Social Hierarchy and Role Communication

Specific means of regulating social/business resources are too numerous to list. I will limit myself to the discussion of two broad categories, *social hierarchy* and *role communication*, which I believe, in tandem with *guanxi* and the Chinese entrepreneurial spirit rooted in pragmatic rationalism, define the nature of the Chinese common cultural/business framework. Social hierarchy and role communication, both of which are humanistic-rationalistic in nature, are as specifically Chinese as *guanxi* and entrepreneurial spirit.

Social Hierarchy. Respect for social hierarchy has been an element of Chinese society as long as Confucianism has defined or contributed toward defining the Chinese way of life. Even under Communism, which vowed to fight for social equality, social hierarchy was never quite removed from Chinese society; it only existed in different forms. Social hierarchy is, in this context, viewed as a Chinese means of regulating social/business resources. This is a concept very different from that of social hierarchy in Western democracies. *In a democracy, a decision is made based on majority votes. In a society where social hierarchy is decisive, one person's voice could prevail over a thousand votes.* Which is the more effective means? The answer is, it depends. *One thing I can say with certainty is that Western democracy hardly has a chance to establish itself in China in the foreseeable future. It would be like pouring oil into water; they cannot become one.* I am neither for nor against democracy, which is neither good nor bad; it is a means. At this stage, China, as a society with a clearly definable social hierarchy which has been in force for thousands of years though it has assumed different forms, will, in my estimation, reject democracy for another fifty years. But the Chinese people definitely need and deserve more liberties and freedom, which is different from the notion of democracy. And having more liberties and freedom does not necessarily mean less respect for social hierarchy. People don't understand that it is not just one hard-liner or two who do not want democracy; it is the people, the Chinese people, who do not feel themselves ready. If you disagree, ask the close to one billion Chinese peasants who until recently never left their land to steal a glimpse of the outside world. The peasants would say, If "democracy" is eatable like rice, give it to me. Ask Chinese entrepreneurs who are now busy making money. If "democracy" is worth one hundred dollars a unit, a capital-hungry manager wouldn't mind owning some. And ask people from other sectors of social life who are struggling to get ahead economically. I guess they won't tell you they want democracy; they want to be rich. Rich first, then democracy, they would say. When the Chinese are thirsty, they still look to Beijing for water. People still feel more comfortable calling their boss "Manager Li" or "Director Zhang" or "Secretary Wang" or simply "Head," since this is still a Chinese society, a very hierarchical one. Let me discuss, very briefly, three issues related to Chinese social hierarchy as a means of regulating social/ business resources: *the role of government; decision-making;* and *social positioning.*

The role of government should never be underestimated in regulating social/business resources in Chinese society. The role of government, when perceived in the context of social hierarchy, becomes the highest level of a certain social system whether you are talking about the central government or a local one. In terms of regulating resources, Beijing has much more power to enjoy and much greater freedom to exercise it than does Washington or probably any other industrialized nation. Arguing which government is better—an authoritarian one or a democratically elected one—misses the point. The point is that if you have any serious business to do in China, you must have the support of the Chinese government at all levels. If the endorsement is lacking from the highest level of the social hierarchy, which is the government, you cannot go too far. All Chinese know that and will work as hard as possible to get it.

Many Chinese willingly seek instructions from their government like children seeking advice from their parents. Government officials, in traditional China, were called *fumuguan,* or "Father-Mother Officials," who were expected to take care of all aspects of a subject's life. What if your "Father-Mother Official" were a corrupt official? You would wait for a cleaner one to arrive to replace him. In present Chinese society, despite the fact that governments at various levels have been suffering from loss of credibility, they are still powerful. People no longer view them as "Father-Mother Officials" from whom to seek advice, but still expect them to take care of all aspects of social or even business life. And this has some serious implications for how business is conducted in China. For example, if there is anything that has gone wrong in your business, your immediate reaction is not to go to a professional to seek advice, but to the government. The government knows this and that's why its bureaucratic apparatus keeps growing at all levels. I am not just referring to the Chinese mainland; the governments in Hong Kong and Taiwan are also implied.

Decision-making in a system that is hierarchically structured may exclude the participation of ordinary system members but it is fast and efficient. Deals that involve billions of dollars can be decided upon within a matter of days, with the participation of only a handful of people at the very top. This can be risky, but can also pay off big in an environment where change is the only constant, and fast decision-making can be crucial. High-speed decision-making is one of the most important ingredients in high-speed management, a fast-growing area of intensive academic inquiry in the United States. It is interesting to note, ironically, that the best high-speed managers are probably not found in the United States. They may well be some Chinese tycoons who know little about the theory of high-speed management but who can say "go" to a billion-dollar deal like throwing a little stone into a pond, with style.

There is an essential difference between a typical Western management system and a typical entrepreneurial Chinese management system. The former is one where decision-making power is in the hands of a CEO chosen by the board of directors and a multiplicity of management layers that report to the CEO or to an appropriate level. The Chinese management system can be solely the design of the owner who, for example, may put his son in the top management position to give him first-hand experience, and the son moves in the direction where his father's eyes turn. There may also be bureaucratic management layers in the latter, but they can be slashed or overpassed any time the father or his son sees fit. Loyalty and obedience from the lower management and employees is expected, and everybody knows that the owner is the decision-maker. As I said above, this can be risky, and the level of risk increases along with the increasing size and complexity of the business and organization. Things are changing though. Western-trained young professionals who are sons and daughters of business owners in Taiwan and Hong Kong are blowing some fresh air into this very much closed decision-making system. For example, Li Ka-shing, a Chinese billionaire based in Hong Kong, has two sons who are both American-trained. It is unlikely that Li's empire will not be influenced by what they've learned in the United States. But Chinese respect for social hierarchy, along with other traditional Confucian values, is so deeply rooted in people's psychology that it won't be swept away by Western managerial practices. I think this tradition will continue to exert its influence on decision-making processes in Chinese businesses and organizations, not just in Hong Kong and Taiwan, but also on the mainland, where state-owned enterprises are being transferred into private or collective hands.

Social positioning refers to how a person is positioned or positions himself or herself in the social hierarchy, which s/he implicitly respects. It's like taking your assigned seat in a theater or a stadium. That's how order is maintained, assuming this is the order that all social members agree to uphold. A culturally respected member in the social hierarchy is one who respects the existing social structure where everyone has a place and is supposed to remain there. It's easy to be told where you stay. It takes an awful lot of social skill and discipline to find your place and go and stay there. The Chinese Communist revolution was one that attempted to destroy the existing social order—quite successfully. But the old social hierarchy was replaced by a new order. The position of emperor was replaced by the chairmanship of the Party. The traditional "Father-Mother Officials" were now Party officials. And so on down the line. The new social order is now fast returning to the old, with modifications and resulting confusions. Whichever order you are in, your position is hierarchically determined. Social hierarchy, tacitly understood among social members, may follow a more complex taxonomy than many of us think. It not only defines how power is shared, but categorizes and then regulates such social/business resources as wealth, age, education, seniority, and experience.

As I said, it is easier to be told what position to take than to find your own position. The real challenge lies in how one learns to take one's position in the social hierarchy in a given system, whether in an organization or in a particular social context. Positioning occurs at different levels: division of labor, task assignment, value congruence, need compatibility, and observance of social rituals. If you don't have the seniority or experience or talent or *guanxi*, you will not ask for a promotion to a senior managerial position; you will stay where you are and be content with your lot. "Let me vacuum the floor. It's my job!" you may say to a colleague in the office who you know is older than you are. Zhou Enlai would always walk a step behind Mao to show his humbleness each time they made a public appearance either in the Great Hall of the People or at the rostrum of Tiananmen. Premier Zhou was never confused about his position in relation to Chairman Mao. Had he been half a step confused, he would have been eliminated like Liu Shaoqi during the Cultural Revolution. All Chinese understood completely the manner in which their premier behaved. Therefore, the observance or the violation of social rituals has serious consequences for determining whether or not one is socially mature. I used to teach at a Chinese university in Shanghai. I knew who I was and my students knew who they were, and we were never confused about our positions. For example, if we walked into a meeting room where there was one soft armchair and all other seats were wooden, the students would almost always seat me in the armchair before they took their seats. This has never happened in my experience in the United States since I came to teach here quite a while ago; students were never culturally programmed to behave that way. Indeed, I would intentionally take a wooden seat to assert equality between professor and students. China and the United States are very different in social hierarchical structure and the handling of it.

Social positioning is closely related to role communication, which is a means by which to reinforce the existing social hierarchy. I will end this chapter with a brief discussion of role communication which I believe characterizes, in addition to *guanxi*, entrepreneurial spirit, and social hierarchy, the common cultural/business framework of the Chinese. Like social hierarchy, role communication is used to regulate social/business resources in a uniquely Chinese way.

Role Communication. Role communication is a process in which people use communication to emphasize each other's role identity. The "I" identity tends to be suppressed in the interaction. According to not a few communication scholars in the United States, only interpersonal communication is quality communication—one where interactants reveal who they are and assert their "I" identity. Role communication, with interactants' individuality suppressed, is superficial. This is a half-truth. To me, role communication is of equal "quality" in China as *interpersonal* communication is in the United States. Indeed, in China as well as in the United States or in any other culture, interpersonal communication cannot occur without interactants playing a certain role, that of parent, daughter, son, friend, lover, speaker, or listener. In the United States, it is possible that when a girl talks with her parents, she is more the individual "Michelle" or "Jennifer" than a daughter. In a typical Chinese family, she talks more from her role of daughter than as a unique self. Which has more quality? To the Chinese, speaking like a daughter when one talks with her parents is more acceptable, hence more qualitative, culturally speaking. Confucius says: behave like a father when you are a father; behave like a son when you are a son. This is the essence of role communication, which, as a ritual, is performed to maintain the existing social hierarchy and further regulate social/business resources.

To make a clearer case, let me take the issue to its extreme. Suppose you are greeting a person who happens to occupy a higher social or organizational position. If this were your section chief, you lean your body a little bit forward to show your humbleness. If this were your division head, you bow 30 degrees. If he were the CEO of your company, you

bow 45 degrees. If, all of a sudden, this person changed to
the governor of your province, you bow further down to 90
degrees. Then, the "last emperor" is standing right in front of
you. Instead of bowing, you kneel down and kowtow to the
ground! This looks like something that happened a long, long
time ago. People no longer bow that much and seldom kowtow unless in a ceremony worshipping one's ancestors.
However, in present-day China, as well as in Hong Kong and
Taiwan, an average Chinese would strive to approximate 30,
45, and 90 degrees, not necessarily by bowing but in other
forms of deferential communication.

Language is a primary tool with which to conduct role
communication. My son has been fast adjusting to the
American way of life in using what I call nondiscriminatory
language in role situations. In a Chinese context, children
learn how to avoid such pronouns as *you* or *she* or *he* or *they*
when they are talking to or referring to their parents. Rather
than saying "What do *you* think?," s/he should say "What
does *Dad* think?" with the father being right there. Now my
son doesn't quite buy that. When he comes home, for example, he might ask Grandma: "Where are *they?*" He means
father and mother. I would insist, if teaching him how to
communicate according to Chinese fashion, that he ask,
"Where are Dad and Mom?" If he is talking to his uncle, he
would have to learn to make role statements like "Would
Uncle have time to have dinner with Dad and Mom" and
"Uncle should take care of yourself."

In formal business situations, I would call, for example,
the manager of a factory "Manager Wang" or "Manager Li"
instead of using his or her given name. In a face-to-face discussion, I would say "Would Manager Wang like me to present
a written proposal?" or "May I have the pleasure of inviting
Manager Li to come to visit with our facility at any time
Manager Li thinks convenient?" In other words, I would try
hard to avoid the use of "you." In China this is called "giving
face" or *gaimianzi*. Face, *mianzi* or *lian*, is an extremely important variable in role communication, in the process of which
you are concerned not only about your own face, but about
another's face. If you fail to give face to another this time, you

risk "losing face," called *diulian*, next time, depending on how serious the situation is. Lin Yutang, a prominent contemporary Chinese scholar, wrote in 1939 in his *My Country and My People* (published by John Day Company, New York):

> Face is psychological and not physiological. Interesting as the Chinese physiological face is, the psychological face makes a still more fascinating study. It is not a face that can be washed or shaved, but a face that can be "granted" and "lost" and "fought for" and "presented as a gift." . . . Abstract and intangible, it is yet the most delicate standard by which Chinese social intercourse is regulated. . . Face cannot be translated or defined. It is like honor and is not honor. It is hollow and is what men fight for and what many women die for. It is invisible and yet by definition exists by being shown to the public. It exists in the ether and yet cannot be heard, and sounds eminently respectable and solid. it is amenable, not to reason but to social convention. (pp. 199–200)

To me, face is more an interpersonal construct than part of a person's psychological entity. Face is a person's public image he or she claims for a set of roles he or she plays. A manager may enjoy being perceived as a generous person while in fact he is a miser, which he himself may know very well. But this public perception is part of his face, and he will fight to preserve it if he decides this is an important social resource of his. One of the most important functions of role communication is to assert one's face and/or give face to another, which is more a performance of a ritual than seeking instrumental goals. A master communicator is one who accomplishes what s/he intends to accomplish and give another enough face so that he or she will be equally happy. This is particularly useful in negotiations in handling conflicts.

In business negotiations with Chinese, a higher-ranking Western negotiator could achieve more than a lower-ranking one not necessarily because the former has better negotiating skills but because the Chinese may give him or her (or, rather, his or her rank) more face. Confrontational and aggressive negotiation styles can be particularly agitating and annoying to the Chinese since such styles are generally deemed to be unsophisticated and subject one to the risk of losing face. The best way to negotiate with the Chinese is never to forget to give face. It almost always pays to send someone whose Chinese counterpart at the negotiation table is a former friend; no matter how tough this Chinese negotiator is, he or she would be willing to give some face to his/her friend. It is a dangerous situation when the face of a Chinese negotiator is completely lost. It is dangerous because he or she may turn around to do whatever is possible to tear your face apart, called *sipolianpi*—and this can indeed be a last resort to restore face. If the American government wants a deal to be had with its Chinese counterpart, and it's a tough sell, send over former President George Bush. He would get more than a nonfriend. That's what *guanxi* is, is it not? Things like what happened in the Yinghe incident on the Indian Ocean in 1993 (in which the United States demanded an inspection of a Chinese ship) can be very dangerous. It was very unusual that the Chinese did not blow up even under the pressure of a whole group of generals in Beijing. That's not a good way to solve conflicts with the Chinese. Nothing can be more ineffective than imposing sanctions on the Chinese to solve a conflict or to make them change behavior. China is big and has enormous space in which to maneuver. Economic sanctions will have little chance to work no matter how punitive. The Chinese would be more concerned about how much face they will lose than about how much business they will lose. And they would retaliate one way or another to tear your face part in order to reclaim their lost face. This part of Chineseness is never quite understood by the West: on the one hand, the Chinese can be extremely pragmatic, so pragmatic that they can become opportunistic; on the other hand, the same Chinese can be extremely sensitive and defensive when it comes to a big face thing, in which case they may want to practice a different kind of rationalism: tear your face apart. It is called in China "attack poison with poison," all for the sake of face.

A concept closely related to face is *renqing*, which I mentioned earlier when discussing *guanxi*. The two-character *renqing* literally means human emotions, though this doesn't quite capture the essence of the Chinese concept. It is more a person's obligations than his or her affections. Obligations in what sense? Let's put it this way. If you once did me a favor, I would feel obligated to pay you back. That means that giving *renqing*, or *gairenqing*, is to invest in face. The one who has received your *renqing* will be expected to give you face like a gift. Psychologically, the Chinese are happier in a position of *gairenqing* (giving *renqing*) than in a position of *qianrenqing* (owing *renqing*). When you are in a position of *qianrenqing*, you're in debt and feel obligated to pay back. When you have given *renqing*, you put another in debt; what you do is to wait for him or her to pay you back. That is another difference between, for example, Chinese and Americans. While Chinese hate to be in debt, in money terms or in terms of *renqing*, Americans live today's life without worrying too much about tomorrow. As long as you can enjoy today, why worry about your debt that is due tomorrow? The Chinese, in contrast, are more concerned about paying back. Life is miserable, they would say, when they are in debt. And it is particularly worrisome if the debt is a kind of *renqingzhai* (*renqing* debt). In other words, what one should do, if one wants to learn to be a sophisticated manager of relationships with the Chinese, is to put his Chinese counterpart in the role of a debtor by giving him or her *renqing*. Once your Chinese counterpart feels he or she is in the role of a debtor, you have the upper hand. Few Westerners seem to have mastered this Chinese art of regulating resources including human relationships. It is no exaggeration to say that to know how to manage roles is to know how to communicate with the Chinese.

The Chinese are, after all, Chinese. They know each other well. If a Chinese from the mainland tells you that he or she could not communicate with his or her compatriots from Taiwan because they are ten times richer, s/he is not being honest or is simply joking. If a Hong Kong Chinese believes the culture of Hong Kong to be more British than Chinese, s/he is probably joking too. Individual Chinese businessmen from Hong Kong, Taiwan, and other parts of East Asia flock to the mainland to invest and trade for all sorts of reasons. But they must share one thing: they can all identify with the common cultural/business framework. It is neither written nor spoken, and yet it's shared. The fact that they share this framework makes doing business much easier, culturally more meaningful, and psychologically more gratifying.

4

Democracy or Benevolent Authoritarianism?

The Master said, Govern the people by regulations, keep order among them by chastisements, and they will flee from you, and lose all self-respect. Govern them by moral force, keep order among them by ritual and they will keep their self-respect and come to you of their own accord.

—The Analects of Confucius

Duke Ting [died 495 B.C.E.] asked for a precept concerning a ruler's use of his ministers and a minister's service to his ruler. Master K'ung replied saying, A ruler in employing his ministers should be guided solely by the prescriptions of ritual. Ministers in serving their ruler, solely by devotion to his cause.

—The Analects of Confucius

Names like Wei Jinsheng, China's most prominent political dissident, make headlines in the West. And such headlines influence public opinion and, almost inescapably, impact on perceptions of decision-makers in the corporate world as well as in the political arena. The annual debate in the U.S. Congress on China's most-favored-nation (MFN) status, for example, had been tied with such headlines for four years until President Clinton took the move to delink MFN with the human rights issue. While Western media reports of China's neglect of individual human liberties and suppression of pro-democracy activities do reflect, though distortedly,[27] a dimension of the reality of China as a nation undergoing radical social changes, they, nevertheless, tend to confuse things and, above all, to solidify preconceived stereotypes and misunderstandings about a country that is so vastly different from their own. Nothing is more obviously convincing than for the media to suggest that to resist efforts to speed up democracy is to resist social progress and therefore represent a moral if not yet a practical challenge to the West. This is easy-to-sell journalism, which, despite its often lack of in-depth analysis of the issue's historical, cultural, and complex "reality" dimensions, has the magic to sway public opinion and political policy considerations in the West. Everyone seems to buy this: Democracy is good; democracy is what China needs now.

The issue is not whether China needs democracy or does not need democracy. The issue is what form of democracy China needs and when. I do not want to imply that China does not need democracy nor do I wish to inject the discussion with value judgments. Let's simply assume, not necessarily based on that Western logic, that China does need democracy—whether a Western type of democracy or a unique Chinese type is another issue. But when? I do not want to make uninformed guesses (it seems that no one, at this stage, can sufficiently be informed on this issue). The safest and most reliable way to say it is let's wait and see, taking the same attitude as "crossing the river while feeling the stones underfoot," which has been a motto for China's reformists for the past decade or so. The prediction I dare venture is let's wait another fifty years and see whether it's too early then to raise the issue of democracy, more seriously than jokingly, in China.

Democracy, Not Yet

First of all, the prevailing mood in present-day China among intellectuals as well as peasants and workers is a preoccupation with making money. Yuan, or yen, or dollar, is the common code that people from all walks of life share. Politics has become a language few Chinese can speak or understand. A typical Chinese peasant would be puzzled and lost for words when asked whether he wanted "democracy." "I want to raise ten more pigs next year," and that's likely to be his answer, which is of course very irrelevant to the question, but very relevant to his immediate living environment. A typical Chinese factory worker would rather go to sleep after having worked extra hours to earn more yuan than discuss the meaning of, for example, democratic elections. Chinese intellectuals, who used to be more politically oriented than their counterparts in probably most other countries, have become very tired of talking about either Marx or Jefferson. Marxism has become antiquated, and democracy seems to belong to the twenty-second century. Many have become more disillusioned than they were before the Tiananmen crisis. Others are preoccupied with their second or third jobs to earn the extra money to make ends meet. Still others pursue their extracurricular activities at the stock exchange. If you could stop any one of them to press for a discussion of democracy, he would, I bet, pretend to be deaf. Every Chinese is talking about money and how to make it. The mood has been there for quite a few years and will continue to prevail in China until everyone becomes "rich." Talking about democracy is like playing piano music to an ox, to use a traditional Chinese proverb: it's too sophisticated a concept for such an unsophisticated audience.

Mainland Chinese have been too poor for too long a time. An average professor teaching in a Chinese university makes no more than 200 U.S. dollars a month if he doesn't work a second or third job, though his living standards have improved compared with five or ten years ago. An average factory worker makes $50–70 a month. People who work for foreign companies or joint ventures can earn as much as $300 a month. Private entrepreneurs can be rich millionaires who could take you to a $500-a-plate dinner without blinking an eye. The number of the superrich on the mainland is small, but they are like popular heroes: people relate their legends as if talking about Red Army veterans during the Cultural Revolution. "If my neighbor is this rich, then why can't I be?" That's the question that everyone is asking. Rarely do they ask, "Why is it that a two-party system is better than one-party rule?" The surest message that I got when I visited Shanghai (after a five-year absence) early in 1994 was that the 1.2 billion Chinese have all joined the most rigorous "Race to Be Rich" known to memory. People simply don't have the time to talk about democracy; they are too busy making money or thinking about how to make it. After having lived in austerity or absolute poverty for forty years, they now realize that it's okay to have money, and one can even feel glorious in becoming rich. The Chinese are still poor, even very poor, compared with the living standards of the more advanced nations. It's their mission today to shake off poverty and claim a more decent human life; democracy is not yet on their agenda.

It's almost impossible for each and every individual living in 20 percent of the world's population which is China today to become rich even over half a century. China, with its limited natural resources, finds it an increasingly fearsome task to merely feed its 1.2 billion people, never mind to attempt to raise their living standards to the level of the world's advanced economies. What's extremely dangerous is the fact that not many Chinese are fully aware of the explosive nature of the population size and the seriousness of the shortage of natural resources. Few seem to be fully prepared, psychologically, for the possibility of unexpected, massive crises such as floods, earthquakes, droughts, and other natural disasters. It is foolish to ignore this in managing a country as vulnerable as China. It is exceedingly difficult for someone born into a more affluent and stable society to understand the sensitivity of the Chinese leadership to the issue of stability in the Middle Kingdom. Mao, Deng, and earlier Chinese rulers would, without exception, warn or be warned of the likelihood of "utter chaos under heaven," called *tian xia da luan.* Whether they were more worried about their power being toppled or about their subjects being thrown into hell is not my concern. What I want to emphasize here is that they did have a reason—a very good one—to worry. You can never expect a regime with such practical worries to experiment wholeheartedly with political reform aimed at democratization of political and social processes, which is, in essence, a redistribution of resources, including power and wealth. Any attempt to loosen social control in the name of practicing democracy would be crushed. I have never had any doubt about that, having lived four decades in that system. This has not only been the practice under the Chinese Communist system. It's been so for the past two thousand years. The suppression of the 1989 Tiananmen rebellion was but a recent example. I would expect any Chinese regime to do the same whenever a similar situation occurs in the future, using whatever measures it considers necessary. It was sheer ignorance on the part of the Clinton administration of the nature of the Chinese political and cultural establishment, to have sent high-ranking officials to Beijing to lecture the Chinese leadership on the issue of human rights and the value of Western democracy. This was like persuading Deng Xiaoping to eat his rice-soup-plus-hot-rotten-bean-curd breakfast with a fork and knife instead of a pair of chopsticks. Deng, if he happened to be in a good mood, would laugh it off with his cute little smile. If he were in a bad mood, he would simply throw the silverware into his spittoon.

China is too large. China is still quite poor. And China needs to raise its educational level. Democracy is based on the free choice of human will. It takes informed argumentation by parities who hold different and often opposing interests to come to a meaningful consensus regarding decision-making. Democratic, free elections based on universal suffrage sound better than having government officials hand-picked by those high up in the power hierarchy. But an uneducated electorate, which is surely the case not only in the vast rural areas in China's inner regions but also among the poorly educated workforce in many of the urban sectors, would be vulnerable and subject to all kinds of political manipulation and abuses. *A feigned democratic system could be worse than an openly declared authoritarian regime because while the nature of the latter is left visible to the whole world, the former could be controlled by a handful of shrewd democratic advocates in name only whose only interest is to get what they want.* There would be no real democracy in the true sense of the word in any society where there has yet to emerge a middle class which provides not only the necessary economic basis, but also an informed electorate capable of decision-making. I do not believe that the nearly one billion Chinese peasants, with an annual per-capita income of less than $300 and a mere elementary or at best secondary education, have developed or will soon develop that capability. They need another two or three generations' effort to develop that capability. It would be simply chaos, or "utter chaos under heaven," if all the Chinese peasants were mobilized to exercise their "democratic rights." That would be the second "peasant revolution," which would be no less chaotic than the one that Mao led and that put the Communist Party in power in 1949.

If a Chinese peasant were granted his right to vote, for whom would he vote? A typical Chinese peasant would vote for his uncle on his father's side or mother's side; he would vote for his aunt on his father's side or mother's side; or he would vote for somebody who shares the same family name and comes from the same clan. He would vote for a member of his innermost circle, his clan, his blood network of *guanxi*. As I discussed in chapter 3, Chinese culture is a culture of *guanxi*, which no revolution—not even the Communist Revolution—ever succeeded in routing out. *This guanxi culture has been so persistently powerful that no political force could design a political roadmap without noting its influence. It indeed has largely undermined the power structure established by the Communist Revolution, at least in the vast rural areas in China.* The Communist Party is still there in China's countryside, but it's not there as an independent political force. It probably never was. It's there as a *hair* attached to the *skin* of the traditional or feudal clan system. The rural clan system, which was very much tied to the land tenure system, was greatly weakened during the various political campaigns after the 1949 revolution, including land reform, collectivization movements, and later communization of rural life, which all occurred in the fifties. The Cultural Revolution of 1966 did not spare the countryside, though the revolution seemed to have inflicted less suffering on the rural peasants than on the intellectuals.

Soon after Deng Xiaoping abolished the commune system as his first large-scale reform initiative in the early eighties and redistributed the land to the peasants, the seemingly dead rural clan system became alive again. The strongest sign of this has been the mushrooming, in the vast rural areas all over China, of lavishly decorated tombs for the ancestors, whose bones were mercilessly dug up by the Red Guards during the Cultural Revolution. Ancestor worship was one of the main pillars of traditional Chinese culture, and its revival in rural China seemed to be the very revival of the rural clan system. It is not that it is occurring today. It happened almost ten years ago. I still vividly remember how I was amazed by a view of the magnificently built tombs around villages in the larger Wenzhou area in coastal Zhejiang Province when I was visiting there back in 1987. This is why I still keep a fresh memory of the scene. As I was driving along a rural highway with a group of local enthusiasts who had arranged for me to do a couple of lectures in the region, I saw some white-painted beautiful houses at the foot of a mountain. "Look at those homes! How beautiful!" I exclaimed. My friends all giggled at my great "professorial discovery." One of them said, "Professor Ju, they are not homes; they are tombs." I wanted to save face and said: "Well, they are homes of the dead." In the homes of the dead resides the spirit of the rural clan system in which all who are alive want to share the same identity by claiming that they belong to the same inner circle. One could never understand the functioning of the local rural governments and Party apparatus without having a full knowledge of the related clan system. They are all one. The Party is in the clan system, and members of the clan are Party members. If you are not yet a Party member, the clan can make you one. It can well be the case in present-day rural China that the village chief concurrently represents the clan whose members use the same family name while managing the local Party branch. The label "Communist" lost its original meaning long ago. It always sounds awkward when the Western media call China "Communist China" or dramatize the nature of joint ventures in China as the teaming up of Western "capitalists" with Chinese "Communists." Who are the "Communists"? Where are they?! The Communist Party is, indeed, no more than a group of privileged power-holders; they could be as capitalistic as Jack Welch or Lee Iacocca. This privileged group can be more feudalistic, and of course, also more powerful, than any other group in rural China. Now you want democracy, and so you want to eliminate the Communist Party. Your head will be cut off if you mean what you say. This is because when you want the Party boss out, very likely you are laying your hand on the head of the clan chief. If you want to impose democracy there (assuming democracy can be imposed) and encourage villagers to elect those whom they trust to be their leaders, the Wangs would all yell "We trust Uncle Wang!" and the Zhangs would all yell back "We want Aunt Zhang!"

It seems that the observable reality together with factors ranging from demographic (a large and very much uneducated populace), to economic (there hasn't appeared yet a genuine middle class), to cultural (revival of the clan system and omnipresence of *guanxi*) supports a view widely shared among Chinese themselves that China will see no democracy in the foreseeable future. The Chinese belong to a different kind of civilization.

Nature of the Party and Why
Benevolent Authoritarianism Is the Way

Now let's take a look at the Party itself and do some content analysis within the political system itself. Again the term "Communist" needs to be clarified. Communism of all stripes has been represented in the long history of the Chinese Communist Party, which was founded in 1921, by such exponents as Dong Biwu, Chen Duxiu, Mao Zedong, Zhou Enlai, Peng Dehuai, Liu Shaoqi, Chen Yun, and then of course, Deng Xiaoping. Most of them are gone. Those who now hold key positions within the Party at the central and provincial levels are those who joined in the revolution in the late forties or early fifties like Party Secretary General Jiang Zemin, Premier Li Peng, and Li's deputy Zhu Rongji. Many were educated in the late fifties or the sixties like the former Party boss of Shanghai, Wu Bangguo, and his successor Huang Ju.[28] *One of the major differences between the present-*

day leadership and the disappearing Red Army generation of Mao's time is that today's group is much less idealogically committed than the early group, whose many members once firmly believed in the ideal of utopian Communism. The present group is much more flexible and pragmatic than their rigid and idealistic predecessors. Nothing is more misleading than to call this group "Communists."[29] They are neither more nor less "Communist" than any other Chinese in mainland China, or in Hong Kong, or even in Taiwan. They are simply a group of power-holders whose instincts as well as informed decisions can influence the future course of Chinese politics.

Another important fact is that the majority of this leadership group have walked a long way to arrive where they now are, having accumulated, over the years, a rich wealth of knowledge of the nature of Chinese society—its economic, political, and social systems. They know what's going on. They know the problems. They know the ills of state-run enterprises. They know the seriousness of corruption among Party and government officials. They know the high stakes involved in economic reform. And they know better than anybody else why democracy can't work in China. They know all of these issues through instinct based on their long years of working their way up the power hierarchy in a highly complex social system of *guanxi* and among a culturally sophisticated people. I have no doubt that they know China better, probably much better, than people like Wei Jingsheng and Wang Dan. They are all seasoned politicians. Apparently, what they know and what they do need not be confused. The nature of the political game is not much of a secret to anybody anywhere. It's very unfortunate that it looked like they needed lecturing by so-called "pro-democracy" elements like what happened during the Tiananmen tragedy of 1989. It was quite unnecessary and the Chinese paid quite an unnecessary price. This is a group of people who do not like to be lectured; nor do they need to be. They know too much already. How much passion, love, concern for their country and people they have left in their hearts is quite another issue. But they definitely know what's important to them and what's not. And they will do what they think is necessary. All efforts designed to persuade them to do otherwise seem to have little chance of succeeding. It cannot be more than exerting political pressure on the Chinese leadership for Western politicians to travel tens of thousands of miles to lecture Beijing on how to run the Middle Kingdom. The effect tends to be more transient than permanent.

The third very important feature about the Communist Party of China is the fact that the Party is home to tens of thousands of Chinese intellectuals, a fact that few China watchers in the West have much knowledge of. One of the paradoxes in Chinese political life is the treatment of Chinese intellectuals. Mao never trusted intellectuals. There was always a peasant in Mao who was a mix of a great poet and an earthy provincial who believed that eating pork fat would nourish his brain. The Chinese Communist Party under Mao undoubtedly should be held responsible for the persecution of hundreds of thousands of intellectuals for more than four decades, beginning with the Yanan Ideological Reformation Period in the early forties. But this is also a Party which has absorbed a great number of intellectuals to serve its needs. Name ten top scientists in today's China and then count how many are not Party members. Name ten top university presidents and count how many are not "Communists," to use a fun term to enliven the copy. And pick randomly one hundred Chinese educated Ph.D.s and count how many have not joined the Chinese Communist Party. The three top exiled Chinese intellectual dissidents—Fang Lizhi, Liu Bingyan, and Wang Ruowang—were all once members of the Chinese Communist Party. Fang is a well-accomplished astrophysicist, Liu an investigative journalist formerly associated with the *People's Daily*, organ of the Chinese Communist Party, and Wang a stingy writer who joined the Party when he was a teen. All three represent the intellectual elite within the Party. We know they have all been kicked out of the Party. But the vast majority of this elite group, those of their kind, remain within the Party.

What does all this mean? It means that when the Party together with seasoned cadres and intellectuals vanishes,

China could be ruled by a bunch of warlords coming out of nowhere who would definitely take advantage of the power vacuum created by the demise of the Party. What happened during the 1966–76 Cultural Revolution—"utter chaos under heaven"—could happen again. People like Wei Jingsheng and Wang Dan may end up having their heads chopped off by the very warlords they supported in the revolt. Then how about a multiparty system? At this time, there does not seem likely to appear a second political party as experienced and powerful as the Communist Party, or able to compete against it. I have little doubt that China's economic reform and the country's stability depends upon the continued existence of the Communist Party. Any major democracy movement, even if not necessarily designed to overthrow the Party, will, however, threaten its continued existence and therefore the country's very much needed stability. The continued rule of the Party may not be the value choice for many Chinese, but it must be there, and will be there probably for a longer time than many people, including Western human rights advocates, would expect.

So the Party will be there, and the continued functioning of the Party depends upon whether or not qualified, "benevolent, authoritarian leaders" can emerge from among the 50 million members of this elite organization. The notion of benevolent authoritarianism suggests that whether or not the Party is in the hands of a handful of benevolent authoritarian leaders is more urgent, at the least for the time being, than a systemic reform in China's political apparatus. Such benevolent authoritarian leaders will be either hand-picked by the power hierarchy or selected as a result of behind-the-door bargaining among various political forces within the Party or a Party branch. If China sees more Bao-the-Judges[30] come onto the country's political stage, the Chinese are lucky. If most of the key positions at the central and provincial levels are occupied by privilege-seeking, corrupt cadres, there will be a second Tiananmen Incident in the not too distant future. Jiang Zemin might have been the best pick by Deng Xiaoping because the former Shanghai mayor has proved to be skillful in maintaining a delicate balance between the

Maoist hardliners and pro-reform liberals, which is key to
ensuring post-Tiananmen stability in the People's Republic.
The fact that benevolent authoritarianism places the picking
of qualified benevolent authoritarian leaders above systemic
reform[31] in the political apparatus implies that such picking
is also nonsystemic or nondemocratic. Hua Guofeng, the
Party chief after Mao, was hand-picked by Mao. Deng
Xiaoping's fall and rise and fall again and then rise again
were all orchestrated by Mao. Hu Yaobang, whose unexpected death triggered the Tiananmen crisis, was put into the
Party boss seat by Deng and then, owing to his too soft a
stance against liberal ideas, dethroned by Deng. Hu was
succeeded by Zhao Ziyang, which was all Deng's decision.
Zhao's sympathetic handling of student demonstrations in
Tiananmen angered Deng, who immediately dumped him.
Then Deng brought Jiang Zemin from Shanghai to Beijing
and decided that Jiang should be the "center of the Party
leadership." Deng has definitely been the most important and
powerful man in the Chinese power hierarchy since the end
of Mao's era. Deng has been as authoritarian as Mao had
been in Party policy design and selection of what used to be
called "revolutionary successors." This may have been a
blessing for China's political, economic, and even cultural
future.

Had there been attempts at radical and comprehensive
systemic political reforms, like those that we have seen in
Russia and Eastern Europe, China may have been engulfed
in civil wars and have had "utter chaos under heaven" for the
past decade. Hu Yaobang, Zhao Zhiyang, Jiang Zemin, and
later Vice-Premier Zhu Rongji (another protégé of Deng's and
another Shanghai mayor)—all have proved to be benevolent
authoritarian leaders; they have contributed to the stability of
a volatile China, first amidst fierce struggles between Maoist
hardliners led by the late Chen Yun and reform-minded mod-
erates under Deng's umbrella, and then after Tiananmen.
Deng has all along been authoritarian; Hu and Zhao were
once authoritarian when they each were in power; and Jiang
and Zhu are no less authoritarian than their predecessors.
But they share another commonality: they have been or were

or are more benevolent than Mao in their handling of state and people's affairs. An objective person would admit that—despite the fact that China has a long way to go to improve its human rights record—the Chinese have become a freer, less poor, and less hungry people in Deng's era. With further development and deepening of China's economic reforms, benevolent authoritarianism will gradually become less authoritarian and more benevolent. And gradually benevolent authoritarianism will pave the way for a carefully designed, step-by-step systemic reform in the country's political institutions. That time will slowly come.

One of the most difficult tasks facing China's leaders, in the next decade or so, is the handling of regionalism which could threaten the very stability of the larger environment needed for furthering the economic reforms. Chang writes:

Contradictions between the center and the lesser regions will worsen in the future. . . . What the leaders in Beijing worry about most is that China's 30 provinces, 300 regions, and 2,000 counties will become the dominions of 30 big princes, 300 medium princes, and 2000 little princes—each pursuing its own course of development, presiding over its own territory, becoming in effect independent kingdoms.[32]

All the contradictions boil down to one central issue: Who gets a larger share of the pie? Each of the 30 provinces, 300 regions, and 2,000 counties, and numerous interest groups began to compete for more resources, more jobs, more market share, more political influence, and a better life for its subjects as soon as the yoke of the absolute equality imposed by a Stalinistic planned economy was thrown off. Taking a look at the latest data on the inflow of foreign direct investment to various places in China (see table 4.1), some big, medium, or little princes would be very happy while others would be ready to fight for their throats not to be cut.

Bejing, in order to prevent a possible disintegration of China into hundreds or thousands of mini-kingdoms, is expected to continue to resort to heavy-handed measures of

Table 4.1. Inflow of Foreign Direct Investment to China
by Destination (1992) (percent of total)

	Contracted	Implemented
Guangdong Provinces	32.4	2.3
Guangzhou City	7.7	5.0
Shenzhen City	4.3	4.1
Jiangsu Province	12.8	13.3
Fujian Province	10.9	12.9
Xiamen	2.9	5.1
Shandong Province	6.7	8.4
Qingdao City	2.0	1.8
Shanghai City	5.0	4.4
Zhejiang Province	4.9	2.1
Ningbo City	2.7	1.0
Hainan Province	3.9	4.1
Total Above	76.6	77.5
Other	23.4	22.5
Total	100.0	100.0

Source: China Newsletter, 105 (July-August 1993): 22–24.

control, even though the effectiveness of such measures is becoming more and more questionable. Beijing's effort to introduce stiffer regimes of taxation to increase its revenue income, is a recent example of how the central government is desperately trying to reclaim part of its lost control. Among other weapons, Beijing is expected to lay a firm hand on two: the People's Liberation Army, the so-called "the barrel of a gun," and the propaganda media, or "the barrel of a pen," which have proved to be of crucial importance for the mainte- nance of the continued functioning of benevolent authoritari- anism. Deng Xiaoping first used the "barrel of a gun" to suppress the Tiananmen uprising. Then the "barrel of a pen" was used to create a social reality to reclaim the legitimacy of the rule and rationality of the bloody suppression. Party Chief Jiang Zemin is also chairman of the powerful Military Commission of the Party's Central Committee whose function is similar to that of a commander-in-chief. The barrel of a gun is expected to continue to be the right arm of the Party; the army will have little chance of being neutralized as long as benevolent authoritarianism is the mode of political rule in the People's Republic. The barrel of a pen also has little chance of becoming a non-Party tool. It will continue to be the left arm of the Party probably for a long time to come. Efforts to push for a free press are bound to fail because the Party will make sure the media remain in its hands. *Indeed, the functioning of democracy will depend, among other factors, upon the neutralization of the military and a free press. When the army is in the hands of the Party and when the press is controlled by the state, the governing regime will be an authoritarian government, as in the case of the People's Republic of China. A benevolent authoritarian government is arguably better than an exploitative authoritarian one, and evidently better for China. It is not yet time for democracy.*

5

Can an Economically Booming China Survive a Systemically and Morally Corrupt China?

The five colors blind the eyes of man;
The five musical notes deafen the ears of man;
The five flavors dull the taste of man;
Horse-racing, hunting and chasing madden the minds of man;
Rare, valuable goods keep their owners awake at night.

—Laotse[33]

Liu Qishan, Fan Zhanwu, Liu Ning, and Yang Mingji had their last dinner on 28 May 1994. The next day, they were each taken to the execution ground to be shot with a bullet in the back of the head. On contraband and bribery charges, the four former Communist Party cadres were found guilty and sentenced to death by the Weihai City Intermediate People's Court in Shandong Province and the Zhuhai City Inter-mediate People's Court in Guangdong Province respectively. The execution was carried out soon after their appeals to the Shandong Higher People's Court or the Guangdong Higher People's Court were rejected. Before their arrest, Liu Qishan was director of the Commerce Bureau of Rushan City; Fan Zhanwu, commissar of the Frontier Inspection Branch of the Weihai Public Security Bureau, and Liu Ning, deputy chief of the Business Division of the same branch, all from Shandong Province. Mr. Yang Mingji was head of the Anti-Contraband Team of the Sanzao Frontier Defense Brigade, Frontier Defense Branch, Zhuhai Municipal Public Security Bureau, Guangdong Province. The four, with other Party and govern-ment officials who received lighter sentences, were involved in a major cigarette contraband valued at 5.17 million yuan. Besides, the four condemned each had accepted hundreds of thousands of yuan of bribes.

Capital punishment for Party and government cadres on serious corruption charges has been frequent since 1989 when the Tiananmen demonstrations were staged to protest, among other matters, the Chinese government's ineffectiveness in preventing corrupt officials from becoming further corrupt. The execution of Mr. Liu and his three comrades-in-arms has been among the most recent. Just a month before, in April 1994, Sung Taifu, president of the Beijing Great Wall Machinery and Electrical Technologies Corporation, was found guilty of embezzlement and bribery and sentenced to death. Mr. Sung was executed on the morning of 11 April after his appeal was rejected by the Beijing Higher People's Court. Mr. Liu's supporter, Li Xiaoshi, vice-director of the State Commission on Science, was expelled from the Party and lost his job. Li was accused of accepting a bribe from Liu. Both the May and April executions received national media coverage. However, despite the Party and government's harsh punishment of corrupt cadres and repeated warning that those who dare to cross the line would have their heads chopped off, the wheels of corruption keep running as if the brake had stopped working. It is expected that more arrests will be made and more heads will be chopped off. But China will remain corrupt, or very corrupt, probably for a very long time, no matter what. This is because, according to some China watchers, China is so corrupt that everyone is corrupted. And the question that lingers on many people's minds is whether or not an economically booming China will survive a systemically and morally corrupt China.

Why Corrupt?

I agree that corruption is a very serious issue in China and has the potential to ruin the whole economic reform program. But the issue warrants a careful study and balanced assessment. First of all, corruption is by no means China's exclusive product. Corruption is found everywhere. It exists, for example, in the New York City police or Tokyo's party politics. Corruption is oftentimes serious in Western Europe. Former Soviet Union and Eastern European countries seem to be as corrupt as China, or more so, in many respects. Many African and Asian military regimes are corrupt, or very corrupt. South America is corrupt in its own ways. In my view, it is extremely hard to judge, either quantitatively or qualitatively, whether China is more or less corrupt than any other country; it seems more acceptable to say that China is corrupt in its unique ways, which must be dealt with seriously. In the same token, to say every Chinese is corrupt is to say every human being is, or at least can be, corrupt.

Second, it is true that every human being can be corrupt. There have always existed three different views regarding human nature. One is that human nature is evil. Another is that human nature is good. Still another is that human nature is indifferent to good and evil, just as water is indifferent to east and west. Mencius of ancient China disagreed with the notion that human nature is neither good nor evil. He said, "Water, indeed, is indifferent to east and west, but is it indifferent to high and low? Man's nature is naturally good just as water naturally flows downward." This is an interesting argument. But can one also say that "human nature is naturally bad just as water naturally flows downward"? Xun Zi, one of the greatest philosophers in ancient China, had this to say: "By nature man departs from his primitive character and capacity as soon as he is born, and he is bound to destroy it. From this point of view, it is clear that man's nature is evil." Xun Zi clearly laid an emphasis on the destructive nature of human desires. I agree that it is a sound argument that such human desires as those for money, power, space, and sex, if unchecked, can be very destructive. Therefore, in this sense, every human being, Chinese or non-Chinese, can be corrupt. May we say that human desires corrupt?

I simply want to emphasize that corruption, which originates from unchecked human desires, is a universal phenomenon: when and where there are human beings, there is the potential for corruption. But contemporary Chinese corruption, as a systemic and moral issue, has occurred in a very unique economic, political, and cultural environment. To understand the corruption issue in China, one must first of all have a good understanding of the economic, political, and cultural nature of that society.

Money Corrupts, but No Money Also Corrupts

First, Chinese corruption has had its economic origin. We often hear people say "Money corrupts." We rarely think about the possibility that "No money also corrupts." And never have we heard people claim that "No money can corrupt even more than money." It seems that the Chinese case has proved that no money also corrupts and no money may corrupt even more than money. I, like many of my contemporaries, grew up in an economic environment in which we had been educated to believe that one could be poor economically but rich spiritually. One might be poor economically and rich spiritually for a while, or even for an extended period of time, but it can be hard to remain in poverty for one's whole life without losing the will to remain "a spiritually rich revolutionary." And it seems almost impossible, judging by what I have seen and heard and personally experienced in the past four decades, that one can be happy to be poor when one sees others, while preaching the virtue of being poor, suck the blood of other people. The Chinese people, due to the enforcement of the Stalinistic economy between 1949 and 1978 (the next year Deng Xiaoping started his economic reforms), had lived too poor a life for too long.

I vividly remember my days back in the early 1970s working on a military farm where I was sent by the government to receive "reeducation," to have my brain washed after my graduation from college. It was hard for me, but I had a great opportunity being exposed to Chinese peasants' life in rural China. I was shocked to learn, because of my then ignorance of the economic conditions in rural China, that an average working peasant's daily income there, in a region where the living standards were not the lowest, was about eight *fen* (roughly four U.S. cents according to the exchange rate at that time). It would not be difficult to imagine how poor the peasants there were at that time. Remember, they were not the poorest. Those who were poorer were people who had to share one pair of trousers among two or three family members. I have traveled around the world and have had exposure to Africa, Asia, Australia, Europe, and North America. And I had first-hand experiences living in one of the poorest regions in Africa. Never have I seen a people as poor as the Chinese peasants. Think of this: As a professor teaching in a major Chinese university, I wasn't even able to make enough to support a family of three. I had to moonlight to make both ends meet. Where did the money go? To the pockets of members of the Chinese Communist Party? I don't believe so. The vast majority of the Chinese Communist Party and government officials were no better than an average Chinese financially, and some of them were even poorer than a peasant. It was unfair to say that they stole the wealth from the people; the system did. It was the Stalinistic economic system that robbed the people of everything they deserved to own.

It might be all right for the Chinese to remain poor and keep feeling "rich" spiritually without being informed that those who lived outside the socialist frontiers, particularly their compatriots in Taiwan and Hong Kong, were living better, indeed, much better. Once the door was pushed open in late 1978, people were stunned by a dazzling array of material goods and the "decadent" lifestyles of the industrial West and the four little dragons—South Korea, Taiwan, Singapore, and Hong Kong—that were brought to their eyes by Western media and incoming tourists. They started to ask questions and feel miserable. The sensation swept across all social classes and touched the heart of each and every Chinese, including members of the ruling Communist Party of China, government officials, workers, peasants, soldiers (the Army no longer seemed interested in "serving the people heart and soul"), and intellectuals. The Chinese, probably for the first time in their life, realized that they did have desires, and did have *the* desire to become a bit richer. The economic reforms that Deng Xiaoping launched in 1979 could not bring money and wealth to the Chinese overnight; the economic system had been laden with too many problems that it could not be fixed within so short a time. But people became increasingly impatient. *When people's expectations were too high to be satisfied and too wild to be controlled, they would try "alternative" means; that was where corruption started.* Who had easy access to these so-called "alternative means?" Those who had power. Who had power? Party and government officials who had the same desire to get rich as fast as any other Chinese individuals, quickly hopped aboard the "alternative means enrichment bandwagon." Alternative means here refer to such practices as backdoor politicking, bribery, embezzlement, and other inappropriate or illegal ways of making money. The people who went so far as to risk their heads being chopped off, like the ones we mentioned at the beginning of the chapter, were typical examples of those who wanted to strike it rich by "alternative means."

The past decade or so has seen an unprecedented exodus of China's top minds to the West, the United States in particular, a phenomenon that has largely been misunderstood. A dominant theory is that the over 40,000 Chinese nationals who are either Ph.D.s or are working on an advanced degree refuse to go back to China because they enjoy the kind of freedom they cannot hope to have in China. This is indeed only half true. It is largely a myth that a scholar or student may risk being persecuted if he or she chooses to return. To me, economy is a bigger factor or predominant factor. I am one of the over 40,000. I chose to stay mainly because I would make one hundred times more money here in the United States than I did in China seven years ago, and I decided that I deserved to make one hundred times more. I knew I should go back. I knew I wouldn't be persecuted if I had chosen to do so. And now I constantly feel guilty about my decision to stay. But I also know life back there for us "pure" intellectuals would be miserably difficult, probably more so than seven years ago, even though the whole economy is booming. Am I corrupt? Maybe, corrupt in the sense that I do not care as much about the destiny of the country any more. And definitely so in the sense that I have become completely alienated from the traditional value of "feeling spiritually clean and elevated while being poor." Lack of money has corrupted me, has it not? But I feel consoled, having convinced myself that at least the "alternative means" that I used were legal and ethical (though maybe marginally so in the eyes of the Chinese government). And I feel more consoled when I believe I am not to blame. Why should I be held responsible for not going back to China? The over 40,000 scholars, Ph.D.s, and students are not to blame. Even people like Liu Qishan whose head was chopped off are not to blame; they have paid the price for their corrupt behavior. It would be unfair to put all the blame on the condemned. If there were a scapegoat, it would be the Stalinistic economic system. It would be "no money." I am really convinced that money corrupts, but no money corrupts too, and utter poverty may lead to utter corruption.

Man Being Above Law Corrupts

Probably the lack of money alone does not necessarily corrupt. But no money plus no rules/laws to follow definitely corrupts. China has been undergoing radical changes in its economic system and to a less extent in its political/legal systems. Old rules, regulations, and laws have become outdated or thrown out or simply forgotten, and new rules, regulations, and laws have not yet taken root. A transitional period like the one China has been going through since Deng started his economic reforms tends to be chaotic, a situation which may present great opportunities for those who want to take advantage of the chaos. Tom Peters published his popular book *Thriving on Chaos* in 1987,[34] where he describes the nature of the world's chaotic business environment. But the title of his book fits so well with the Chinese situation that it exemplifies exactly what Peters intends in differentiating between the prepositions "amidst" and "on." He says, "To thrive 'amidst' chaos means to cope or come to grips with it, to succeed in spite of it. But that is too reactive an approach, and misses the point. The true objective is to take the chaos as given and learn to thrive *on* it." Politicians, power mongers, and corrupt officials are happy to see the chaos prolong itself, which is undoubtedly to their advantage. Many seasoned

Chinese Party and government officials at the central, provincial, and county levels have already benefited from a chaotic decade of transition, not in the sense that China's economic life has become more orderly, but in the sense that the chaos has given them the kinds of opportunities they had never imagined in the pre-reform years. And I daresay not a small number of them just wish the chaotic transitional period will last a bit longer. People may feel sorry for the contrabandist Mr. Liu Qishan and others who were singled out for execution to be examples of "killing a chicken to warn a group of monkeys" or "executing one to warn a hundred." Hundreds of thousands of corrupt "monkeys" seem to have escaped punishment because they've learned to "thrive on chaos" so well. Mr. Liu and the other condemned were just little chickens; unlike monkeys, they were not privileged to enjoy protection and support from some powerful and untouchable Monkey King.

Rules, regulations, and laws are enacted to ensure an orderly economic, political, and social life. They are also standards for appropriate and legal economic, political, and social behaviors. Theoretically, they represent major barriers to those who want to cross the line. But rules, regulations, and laws are all created by humans, and it follows that humans can choose the means by which to carry them out or to bypass them. Indeed, there have been enacted countless laws and decrees, rules and regulations in various fields in the People's Republic since 1978. But who cares? *In present-day China, man is still above the law.*[35] *Laws exist, but they are not necessarily enforceable.* Take traffic rules, for example. In China, as here in the United States, you must stop your car before a red light. But, in China, who cares?! In January 1994, I paid a visit to Shanghai and saw the most chaotic traffic on earth. To many drivers, it didn't matter whether it was red light or green light or no light, particularly at intersections where there were no traffic police. They obeyed no rules; they wrote their own rules.

Since rules, regulations, and laws are in the hands of those who occupy various Party or government positions, they enjoy great leeway in terms of how to interpret them, when, where, and for whom they apply. There seems to have been constructed a tightly knit network of mutual protection. Once one is in this circle of mutual protection, one can safely go corrupt. That's why corruption has become such a serious issue with Party organizations and government agencies at all levels. As is known to us all, Party and government corruption was one of the main factors that caused the Tiananmen crisis. It was triggered by the 15 April death of liberal Party Chief Hu Yaobang and climaxed on 3–4 June when tanks rolled into Tiananmen Square. *Unfortunately, Tiananmen was too high a price for the Chinese to pay. There has been little progress ever since in checking the tide of corruption. It is unstoppable because there has not been established a mechanism with which to enforce rules, regulations, and laws.*

The mechanism refers to that which enforces checks and balances among the subsystems within the larger economic and political system of the People's Republic. *In China, there are kingdoms within larger kingdoms within still larger kingdoms, each of which is a tightly knit network of mutual protection.* Neither in theory nor in practice does checks and balances mean anything to Party and government officials or to the People's Liberation Army. For example, who dares to touch the People's Liberation Army (PLA)? The military-run businesses, or PLA Inc., represent more than 20,000 enterprises in everything from telecommunications and transport to mining and massage parlors. They use their connections in civilian governments, the police, and the tax bureau to get what other people cannot get through normal channels including, of course, nonpayment of taxes. The Guangzhou Military Region Command property developer, for example, has not paid any income tax since it was set up in 1985, and it has since renegotiated another three years' tax holiday. Military-run enterprises also skirt the law by using duty-free import permits reserved for the PLA to bring in products for resale. And some military profiteers violate the law outright by smuggling anything from cars to cigarettes to computers to China. And nobody can touch them. What the PLA Inc. can do, Party and government officials can do too as long as they have established their own "state within a state" or "kingdom within a kingdom," where they all have their own "laws" to enforce.

No Morals Certainly Corrupts

No money corrupts. Man being above the law corrupts. And no morals certainly corrupts. I mentioned in earlier chapters that Godwin Chu and I did a major study in the larger Shanghai area in the late 1980s investigating cultural change patterns in contemporary China. We wrote in our co-authored *The Great Wall in Ruins: Communication and Cultural Change in China*:

> In northern China, starting at the ancient battle-ground near Fort Shanhai and stretching across wind-swept expanses of virgin mountains and empty deserts nearly all the way to Mongolia, lies the Great Wall.
>
> For centuries Chinese were sheltered by another Great Wall. This was not a wall of stones and mortar, but a wall of symbols and ideas, of traditional values and beliefs, that stood just as firm and strong in the minds of Chinese. This cultural bulwark held Chinese society together for millenniums, shielding Chinese life from external encroachment and internal erosion.
>
> It was during the reign of Chairman Mao Zedong that Chinese people, inspired by his idealistic concept of a Communist utopia and propelled by his charismatic leadership, participated in a prolonged and traumatic process of radical social transformation. For the first time in history, traditional Chinese culture was forced to undergo major changes of unprecedented dimen-sions, all within a short span of decades.
>
> The cultural Great Wall is in ruins. Traditional values, beliefs, and morals have been torn apart while a new culture has yet to be formulated. Chinese people have been living in a cultural void since the Cultural Revolution came to its end in 1976. *Culture is that which injects order and structure to society where its members are taught to behave using cultural*

values, beliefs, and morals as standards. The worst thing that can happen to a culture is having no values, beliefs, or morals for its members to follow. People were not happy, but life was structured during the long Mao era between 1949, the year when the People's Republic was founded, and 1976 when Mao passed away, even including the years of the Cultural Revolution. This is because the Chinese still believed in something, utopian Communism, for example. In the preface of this same book, *The Great Wall in Ruins: Communication and Cultural Change in China,* there is a passage that describes this author's behavior and psychology during the Cultural Revolution:

> While he could not understand what was happening right in front of him, he often followed the then popular processions of parades showing support for Mao and madly shouting "Long Live Chairman Mao!" Like Lu Xun's "Ah Q,"[36] he just could not stand the idea of being left out of the revolutionary process no matter how little he understood it.

I have to admit that during my youth in the disastrous Cultural Revolution, I did have values, beliefs, and morals I held as sacred. I shared the Party diction that "living in poverty while feeling spiritually elevated" was a virtuous value. I believed that socialism was a better social development model than capitalism. And I felt psychologically gratified when I sacrificed for the good of the country because I had been educated to believe that that was moral behavior. Life was hard, but I never went morally "corrupt." Then came the period of Deng's economic reforms. It was really a second emancipation for the Chinese people, an emancipation from the ideological yoke of Maoism. Gradually, such ideologies as class struggle theory, utopian Communism, and, of course, "eating out of the same big pot," were cleansed from people's minds. Everything came so abruptly, and the changes were so fundamentally radical that few Chinese were able to put into context what was going on. Now traditions were gone (they had been swept away as early as during the 1966–76

Cultural Revolution), and Maoism became a new page in the history book. All of a sudden, the Chinese, who had lived an ideology-intensive life so long under Mao, became empty-headed, without soul, and amoral. Like millions of fellow Chinese, I myself became completely disoriented. I experienced utter pain when I was writing the following auto-biographical passage: "[T]he Tiananmen killings of 1989 smashed his last dreams to pieces. He now lost all hope, his last hope. And he also lost his cultural identity. He felt dead as a cultural being."[37]

It was a painful experience for me because I knew having no soul and moral compass is very close to going corrupt. I admit I did become corrupted, not in a metaphorical sense, but in the sense of the real meaning of the word even though I should not be held responsible for going corrupt. For example, instead of going back to China to serve as originally planned after I completed my research here in the United States, I stayed. I stayed not because I was afraid of political persecution; I wouldn't be persecuted since I had always been a moderate as far as my political views were concerned. I stayed because I did not care about the people who raised me any more. Nor did I care about the destiny of my students, colleagues, and friends any more. All I was concerned about was my future, my success, my happiness. Me became my soul, my moral, my world. Though I didn't rob or steal, nor was I involved in any unethical behavior, but I let loose the destructive nature of my inner human desires that had long been under moral control.

If an amoral person lived in poverty and in a social environment where man is above the law, he or she would be very vulnerable to corruption. And this has been the case for many ordinary Chinese as well as those who have power. To me, it is always insufficient to argue that corruption has been running rampant in China because the ruling Communist Party and government have been ineffective in punishing the corrupt. *No checks and balances mechanism or insufficiently established rules, regulations, or laws should be held responsible; for the weakening of morality in society has also been the major reason for mass-scale corruption in China.*

It seems clear that China's economic, political, and cultural environment has been a hotbed for corrupt behavior. Therefore, to solve the corruption problem in China, one cannot just "execute one to warn a hundred," which can be effective for only a short period. More fundamental work needs to be done. This leads us to the question: What needs to be done in order for an economically booming China to survive a systemically and morally corrupt China?

What Needs to Be Done to Solve the Corruption Problem?

Since no money corrupts, so make people rich. Since man being above the law corrupts, make laws enforceable. Since no morals corrupts, bring back morals to the people. I believe that, working hard in these three areas, things will improve gradually. And finally an economically booming China will survive a systemically and morally corrupt China.

Step 1: Economic Development

As I wrote earlier, the Chinese have been living in poverty for too long, and they all wish to live better, or at least to live like decent human beings with enough food to eat, enough clothes to wear, and reasonable space in which to live. Deng Xiaoping's economic reform program, which was started in the late 1970s, seems to be bringing hope to one-fifth of the world's population. Despite the fact that the gap between the rich and the poor is fast widening, the living standards of the general populace have been improving. Though poor, and in some cases very poor, in general the Chinese have more money than in the past. Take individual Chinese savings, for example. A record total of 12,000 billion yuan was registered in 1993 by all Chinese individuals residing in the People's Republic (about 140 billion U.S. dollars at the exchange rate of $1 equaling 8.6 Chinese yuan), of which 33 percent were the savings of urban residents, 26 percent belonged to the peasants, 28 percent were those of the self-employed, and the rest was held by others. Based on this statistic, an average Chinese had 900 yuan (a little bit more than $100) in savings in 1993. Still a picture of a big China

($140 billion) versus poor Chinese (about $100 in savings). But this is already encouraging since the Chinese never had this much money to put in the bank before.

Instead of preaching the virtue of "remaining poor while feeling spiritually elevated," the Chinese government has designed a plan to be executed between now and the end of the twentieth century in order to elevate—not spiritually but economically—the remaining 80 million Chinese from poverty. The plan targets the poorest regions with a view to raising the level of economic and social development and narrowing the gap between the relatively prosperous east coast and China's poor interior in the west. To what extent China's economic development will help alleviate its corruption problem can hardly be quantified in a scientific way, but I am sure the role of economic development will be positive. A relatively solid material basis is not only a necessary precondition for democracy, but can also be a damper of corruption.

Step 2: Gradual Systemic Reform under
Benevolent Authoritarianism

China's economic reforms, particularly in the area of state enterprises, are deepening, albeit with a high price and at the risk of alienating and angering millions of state workers who may lose their jobs to the more competitive joint-ventures or collectively owned businesses. Political reform has been a sensitive topic since the Tiananmen incident in 1989, but gradually, along with the deepening of the economic reforms under benevolent authoritarianism, it will be put on the agenda with some items getting priority handling. More touchy issues such as one-party rule versus multiparty politics are put aside for future treatment. This is undoubtedly going to be very difficult since the very nature of benevolent authoritarianism resists top-to-bottom systemic reform. *The main contradiction will be the practice of rule by man and that of rule of law. The contradiction may be reconciled under benevolent authoritarianism. A more feasible approach, at this stage, seems a combination of both rule by man—a good man, hopefully—and rule of law.*

The term "systemic reform" is meant to be inclusive of reform in all major social institutions: economic, financial, political, legal, educational, media, and so on. The key to successful systemic reform under benevolent authoritarianism is China's Party and government officials who have been the target of popular accusations for their corrupt behavior. Many of them have certainly taken advantage of systemic imperfections and have abused their power and public resources to serve their own purposes. I don't think it helps too much to speculate on major breakthroughs in reforms in China's political system and other systems. To me, it is more important, under China's current circumstances, to build a whole new generation of cadres armed with the knowledge of laws, well disciplined, and trained to protect the integrity of the legal system. *Having rules, regulations, and laws is no different than having none of them if they are not enforceable or if their enforcers are absent.* The cadres who are entrusted to maintain an orderly economic, political, and social life must make sure, first of all, that they themselves do not go corrupt. Then, and only then, can they become the guardian of a systemically clean society.

Step 3: Moral Education

Confucianism has been torn apart. Maoism is largely gone. Western values and lifestyles keep creeping into China together with Hollywood movies, MTV, Coca-Cola, and McDonald's. The first question that one needs to ask is what morals do the Chinese need? Confucian virtues? Not really. Maoism? Almost impossible. Western values and moral standards? Well, they belong to the West. Or a little bit of the positive from each of the three moral codes? Whatever the case, the Chinese need to create a new moral system to fit with the changed social environment, something with which the Chinese can identify and behave accordingly.

The next question is how to carry out *effectively* the moral education of 1.2 billion people. A government-led propaganda campaign could be very effective in destroying the old, as it was during the Cultural Revolution, but has never been quite so effective in establishing the new. This seems the very reason why the cultural or moral void has never quite been filled since the early 1980s when Deng started his economic reforms. For example, China's model Party and government official Jiao Yulu, the late Party secretary of the Lankao County Committee, Henan Province, died of cancer thirty years ago. He has since been praised as having given his whole life to the Lankao people who happened to reside in an extremely poor region. During his approximately 400 days in Lankao, Mr. Jiao walked to all the villages of the county and worked as hard as he possibly could (he knew he had cancer and his days were numbered) in order to bring hope to the people of Lankao. Jiao was recognized as being honest and upright in carrying out his official duties and never sought private gain for his family members or himself. I was a teen when Jiao's deeds were publicized by the propaganda media, and we were deeply moved by his selflessness as a public servant. At a gathering organized by the Henan Provincial Party Committee on 14 May 1994 to mark the 30th anniversary of Jiao's death, Politburo member Hu Jintao, taking advantage of this important opportunity, called on all the Party members and government officials to learn from Jiao Yulu his spirit as a public servant. Alas, thirty years have passed since Jiao passed away, and there has still been only one lonely Jiao Yulu. Not many Party and government cadres followed his example despite the Party and government's continuous propaganda effort; if they had, there would not have been such a serious corruption problem plaguing the Party and government at all levels. To me, *propaganda won't help too much. China simply needs many more honest and upright cadres from the very top in Beijing to the very bottom in a rural village. This reconfirms my earlier suggestion that China needs a whole new generation of well-educated, well-disciplined, and well-trained cadres. One living example will be more effective than endless propaganda.* So how to carry out moral education among 1.2 billion people? Simple: show the people more *honest and upright* living examples from among millions of cadres.

Moral education at the mass level can well start from within the family. The work-unit-organized Friday afternoon study group was, like media propaganda, never an effective moral education forum. I cannot remember how many hours

I once spent with the study group, but I remember one thing: I never learned anything practically useful except how to live a double-faced organizational life. Family, to me, would be one hundred times better than a work-unit-organized study group since within the family people tend to speak their heart and feel less threatened when they tell the truth. Besides, in contemporary Chinese families, there still exists respectful authority even though it is being weakened. When and where there is authority, one listens, which is so important for moral education. One of the most important findings in our co-authored book *The Great Wall in Ruins: Communication and Cultural Change in China*, is the fact that the Chinese family unit, despite the havoc of the ten-year Cultural Revolution, remains solidly stable. The Chinese family has been a rare oasis of individual privacy, trusted relationships, and moral integrity within the cultural Great Wall now very much in ruins. I now have a dream: *the rejuvenation of Chinese culture, including moral education, may well start from within Chinese families. The Great Wall is ruins, but not the Chinese family.*

Church can otherwise be an available institution for moral education, but religious life has never been essential for the Chinese for the past two thousand years. However, a young Chinese person's school life is definitely a more crucial factor in his or her moral education. Education, not just moral education, but education in general, holds the key to the rise of the Fourth Power and the continuous prosperity of the 1.2 billion people. This will be the topic of the next chapter.

The three steps need not be taken separately; they are indeed linked together as an interlocked system. I believe that if the three steps are seriously followed and executed, an economically booming China can certainly survive a systemically and morally corrupt China. China is big. Any big problem China is faced with may take time, and probably a long time, to solve.

Occasionally, we may still expect the head of another Liu Qishan or Wang Qishan or Zhang Qishan to be chopped off. Punishment, including capital punishment, is necessary and can be effective for a short period of time. But punishment cannot uproot the corruption that has been a logical result of China's unique economic, political, and cultural environments, in whose improvement lies the key to solving China's corruption issue.

6

Education Holds China's Future

Study well, and make progress every day.

—Mao Zedong[38]

I myself was an educator as well a student who experienced so much in my native country China. Given my unique experiences, instead of doing a scientific survey of the historical background of the educational system of the People's Republic, I wish to tell two separate and yet related stories about myself, first as a student and later as a professor, during a span of over three decades.

A Tale of Two Roles—Student and Professor

As a Student

I considered myself China-educated, though I did part of my advanced graduate work at the State University of New York, Albany, in the United States and earned my Ph.D. in political science at the University of Belgrade in Yugoslavia. I was a graduate of the English Language and Literature Department of Fudan University in 1969, and earned my master's degree in Fudan's Journalism Department in 1981. I was a hardworking and obedient student, a pious follower of Confucian ethics, a marginal believer in Marxist and Maoist doctrines. *As a young student, I learned all three: (1) Marxist and Maoist doctrines (more from school and the social media than from home); (2) Disciplinary knowledge—humanities and sciences—(mainly from school); and (3) Confucian morals and behaviors (more from home than from school and the social media).*

I was finishing my primary schooling in 1957 when Mao launched the Anti-Rightist Campaign,[39] a watershed political event in contemporary Chinese history since China's superstructure at that time, including its educational system, became increasingly politicized and confusing to a teenager like me. I was definitely too young to understand what was going on in the political life of the People's Republic. During my first year of junior middle school, I, together with my schoolmates, learned how to "make steel" in a steel factory as part of our required contribution to Mao's "Great Leap Forward." (Mao called on the whole nation to participate in "making steel" so we could catch up with industrialized Great Britain within fifteen years.) I had fun working night-shifts like a grown-up; in what ways I was contributing to Mao's revolution I didn't care or didn't know how to care. I was only twelve years old. Gradually, politics was creeping into the school curriculum, into the way that schools were managed, and how teachers and students were rewarded and punished. But I was still too young to understand. I simply listened to my teachers, as I was told to do by my parents. "Teacher" was the most knowledgeable and most respected person in my mind; anything teacher said or did I was supposed to follow. Any form of questioning would be inappropriate. I learned—from whom I learned this I don't know—that it was morally wrong to question or challenge one's parents, and it was more so to do this to your teacher. Learning how to respect parents and teachers was one of the most basic and important ethical norms in Chinese society, and one needed to learn it early on. School discipline, as an institutionalized custodian of learning, was strict and unchallengeable, and I, like most of my peers, behaved. My school was one hour's walk away from home. I had to get up early so that I wouldn't be late for school (I would feel like I had committed a horrible error if I failed to arrive at school on time). Mother would give me ten cents to buy bus tickets, but I would always choose to walk so that I could return the money to Mother. Strangely, I never felt life was miserable; I thought life was supposed to be that way. With ethical values rooted early on in my psychology due to family and school education, I was able to study hard and earn good grades. I studied hard to earn good grades because I knew that would make Mother and Father happy; I thought that was what a dutiful son was supposed to do. It was not for the sake of expanding my knowledge, nor was it for the benefit of the country; it was for the parents. I had the greatest gratification from a smiling face of Mother or Father as they saw my grade report. At that time, the notion of elective courses was alien not only to us students but also to teachers. All courses were required if it was the school arrangement. I was lucky to be placed in an English class for my foreign language requirement. Most classes at that time were required to study Russian. It was all the government's decision; neither students nor teachers had a choice. School life was strictly hierarchical, and no questioning was allowed or expected. We never did ask questions, and never even considered asking why.

As a result of Mao's "Great Leap Forward" and "People's Commune," China was experiencing a famine in 1961 when I was enrolled in the prep school of Shanghai Teachers' College. Political control was tightened for fear that voicing resentment against Mao's revolutionary experiments could trigger major social upheavals. For the first time in my life as a student, I experienced a fearsome feeling: I felt there was a big eye behind me watching not only what I did but also what I thought. I daresay this was a kind of feeling no American high school students could possibly identify with. It was a unique feeling only people who happened to have lived in that environment could meaningfully relate to. Though I did not have a full understanding of Mao's theory of class struggle that was the talk of the state's propaganda machines, I knew if I did not side politically with the Party, I would be lumped into the camp of "class enemies," which would mean the end of my career, end of my dreams, end of my relationship with my family members, the end of everything. I nervously felt I might be very close to that camp because one of my compositions had been singled out as an example of "bad bourgeois taste." I thought it was a big offense, and I was edging close to the camp of "class enemies." Almost overnight, I became politically conscious of the larger social and political environment. I was fifteen years old. I and my fellow Chinese who happened to belong to the same generation became very precocious politically, which shattered our youthhood dreams too early. It was sad that China's educational system was fast becoming an arm of the political apparatus. But this is important to record, nevertheless, since it has had important implications on the psychological and political making of the whole generation that I belong to. Despite the wanton politicization of school life in pre–Cultural Revolution China, serious academic study was still emphasized and Chinese families continued to exert their influence on their children in terms of reinforcing traditional Confucian values, now often within the space of home.

The Cultural Revolution started in 1966, two years after I entered college. The 1966–76 Cultural Revolution was a revolution designed to uproot from the soil of the People's Republic anything that was "cultural." Disciplinary knowledge—the humanities and the social sciences—was "cultural," and so had to be discarded. Traditional values, beliefs, and behavioral patterns were also "cultural," and therefore had to be criticized. What remained for students to study at school was Marxist and Maoist doctrines. As if watching scenes of a horror movie, I was terrified to see professors getting beaten up, books burned, fellow students condemned as reactionaries and forced to commit suicide. I described myself in *The Great Wall in Ruins*:

> While he could not understand what was happening right in front of him, he often followed the then popular processions of parades showing support for Mao and madly shouting "Long Live Chairman Mao!" Like Lu Xun's "Ah Q," he just could not stand the idea of being left out of the revolutionary process no matter how little he understood it. Soon he traveled to Beijing. He remembers he felt he was the happiest person on earth when he saw Chairman Mao standing in a military jeep reviewing the Red Guards in Tiananmen Square even though he knew he was not supposed to be there

because of his non-membership in any Red Guard organization.[40]

Judging from the above passage, it is not difficult to conclude that China's educational system changed its very nature of education during the ten-year Cultural Revolution; it was one of the darkest pages in the history of human civilization. It is important to remember that it is against this historical background that I am talking about the possibility of reviving and reforming China's educational system.

College graduates, Red Guards and non–Red Guards alike, soon found themselves betrayed by the revolution they so naively and yet wholeheartedly supported. They were all sent to military farms or remote villages to receive what Chairman Mao called "reeducation." Such reeducation was positive in one sense: we were provided with an opportunity, albeit a painful one, to get exposed to the real life of rural peasants, who, more than any other social class, defined the nature of contemporary Chinese society. I felt I was able to understand China better after I had had one and half years' hard labor on a military farm in Anhui Province. I was fortunate (and unfortunate) to be able to experience first-hand the ten-year Cultural Revolution which has become one of the darkest pages in China's history.

As I wrote earlier, I learned three things: Marxist and Maoist doctrines; knowledge of humanities and sciences; and traditional Chinese values, beliefs, and behaviors. And I learned them at school, in society, and from parents and other family members. Reflecting back, I feel all of them have been useful, not just the disciplinary knowledge and the normative teachings of Confucianism, but also Marxism and Maoism, the knowledge of which helped me survive during a time when every aspect of the nation's social life, including education, was politicized. In a sense we might be considered more mature politically and culturally than succeeding generations because of the education and "reeducation" we received over a two-decade period (1958–78) that was crisscrossed by the many political campaigns that Mao launched, including the 1966–76 Cultural Revolution.

Deng called for China's economic reforms in 1978, the year I returned to Fudan to do my graduate work after an eight-year absence from academic life. My role soon changed from student to teacher; this occurred during Deng's reform years. Mao had educated me, and I was now helping Deng educate others.

As a Professor

Soon after I returned to Fudan University in Shanghai from the State University of New York, Albany, where I studied communications, I was appointed head of the university's international journalism program designed to train journalists for the official Xinhua News Agency. The program was the first of its kind in the People's Republic. With support from Beijing and within the university, I was able to amass a group of first-class instructors, many of whom were younger than I was, though I was called "a young communications scholar" in local newspaper articles that featured our program. I had some wonderful years working with my colleagues and seeing my students launch their careers in Beijing. According to the dean of Fudan's school of journalism at that time, a well-known essayist based in Shanghai, one has to be good at *er dian yi bi* ("two classics and one pen") in order to work for Xinhua News Agency, China's largest news organization. He meant the "classics" to be Marxist/Maoist classics and traditional classics. "One pen," to him, was one's writing skills. By emphasizing both "Marxist and Maoist classics" and "traditional classics," he put himself in a dilemma in which most Chinese educators at that time found themselves trapped since the two could hardly be reconciled. Traditional classics—and the values behind them—were attacked during the Cultural Revolution, but they were making their way back into society. Marxist and Maoist doctrines were still recognized as dominating political codes, though in a much milder way than during the late sixties and early seventies. They became increasingly weaker until after the Tiananmen Square incident of 1989, which poisoned the educational as well as political climate almost overnight. What had really been troubling to us educators and students alike had been the inflow of

Western values and way of life since 1978, when Deng decided to open China's door to the outside world. Ever since China's door was first forced open by British gunships in the Opium War of 1940-42, its people became vulnerable and unsure about themselves in the face of any major foreign intrusion either in the form of military invasion or in the form of ideologies and values. Marxism was a unique form of Western ideological invasion into a then semi-feudalist and semi-colonial China, and the invasion was so thorough and effective that Marxism became the dominating ideology of the world's largest population for three decades. The recent Western invasion, which started in the early eighties and is becoming irresistible for the Chinese, young Chinese in particular, has been in the form of Hollywood movies, Levi jeans, Coca-Cola, and McDonald's, or, more succinctly, the American way of life as the sum of individual freedoms plus dollars. Neither of the two invasions, Marxist invasion or Western capitalist invasion, should be seen as right or wrong; instead, both should be examined in their unique historical context. However, two general conditions can be cited to explain why the two invasions occurred the way they did. One is poverty; the other, the lack of education on the part of the populace. *The weakest human being on earth is one who has neither material means for physical survival nor nutrition for mind and heart for spiritual self-support. A strong nation is one where people are entitled to enjoy both.* Deng Xiaoping seems to understand this better than any of his comrades-in-arms in the political hierarchy. But time is not on his side when it comes to education; it would take too long a time for the 1.2 billion Chinese, or just one-tenth of them, to be educated. Deng needs immediate economic returns and he is achieving them at the cost of mass education, at least for the time being. In the meantime, he seems to have accepted, albeit reluctantly, the second Western invasion, the Western capitalist invasion Mao once vehemently rejected.

As a professor in a major Chinese university, I witnessed how Marxism gradually lost its appeal for the top minds of the nation, and how the "demon" of Western materialism crept into the dreams of our students, young faculty members, and finally myself. I saw, with my own eyes, how China's higher education proceeded, step by step, into a dead end. It was a sad and painful realization that I, one of the millions of beneficiaries—or products even, of China's educational system—finally rebelled and betrayed it. The open-door policy and economic reforms that Deng has endorsed were supposed to inject new blood into China's educational system. Quite the contrary, it has resulted in the loss of thousands upon thousands of the nation's first-class scholars and scientists to the United States and other industrialized countries. Many of those who remained on college campuses in China later found consolation in stock markets, import and export businesses, and other nonacademic spheres. Mao's revolution had created millions of rigid minds. Deng's revolution has been turning a large portion of these rigid minds and later joined younger minds into a huge "Chinese Intellectual Diaspora" scattered around the world, including over 40,000 in the United States alone. Many more do battle in domestic commercial enterprises. Those who joined neither camp are stuck in university labs or classrooms in the People's Republic making $100 a month.

During my tenure as director of the international journalism program of Fudan University between 1984 and 1988, I let all those talented members of my group go, one by one. Most of them are now in the United States. Many of them would say they really did not want to go; they had simply been blown out by the wind of Deng's open-door policy and economic reforms. "I wouldn't go," I said to myself. But soon I thought it was my turn when I found myself a lonely "commander" of myself. I packed up and left China on 4 July 1988, and became, most reluctantly and not without deep feelings of guilt, one of too many that China lost. Never in the history of China or of any other country has there been a collective intellectual desertion on such a massive scale! Even if the deserters, including myself, deserve a moral sanction, there must be either something wrong or unavoidable for this to happen.

What's wrong? Or what's unavoidable?

Let me make a few speculations. First, the system didn't seem to have properly treated the country's minds. Second, the Chinese intellectuals had lived too poor a life for too long a time; many thought that to turn down a $50,000–60,000 job offer would now be sheer stupidity. Third, China's top priority has all along been economic development; education, which doesn't reap immediate rewards, is expendable. Fourth, because the future of China's universities appears equally bleak and without reform, going back to teach in China would be suicidal, many would think.

How to correct it?

It would be no use calling for a quick fix in the educational system; it's been an age-old problem. It would be no use complaining; the state has no money to give professors for pay raises that would approach the lowest international standard. And it would be catastrophic to go to the streets to protest; Deng Xiaoping would send armed police to arrest you. But this doesn't mean Beijing can wait another decade with its arms folded. If I had an opportunity to talk to my former mayor Jiang Zemin, I would tell him to put two words on China's top priority list: economy and education, assuming he has consolidated his power base in the military. I am here to offer neither prescriptions or recipes; I do not think I know more than most of my Chinese colleagues about the current educational system since I have not been a resident professor in China for over seven years. But I do feel, as a student and educator with decades of first-hand experiences, that China's road to the twenty-first century lies in its sustained economic growth and a matching educational system. If I were allowed to make an extreme statement, I would say it is education that holds the key to China's future.

Why Does Education Hold the Key to China's Future?

To me, this is a short-term economic as well as a long-term cultural question. As the economic reforms deepen and the nation's industries go from low-tech to mid-tech to high-tech, millions upon millions of educated and skilled workers will enter the workforce alongside the demand for an enormous number of first-class natural and social scientists, given the size of China's economy, to sustain the functioning of the nation's basic and applied research establishment. *Basically, three types of education will be needed: (1) education that produces skilled workers for various industries; (2) education that trains engineers and professionals such as managerial personnel, financial experts, lawyers, teachers, computer programers, international traders, and translators; and (3) education that offers the nation world-class scholars and scientists.* It is inconceivable that China will be able to sustain its close to double-digit annual GDP growth for another five to ten years without significant progress toward all three educational objectives. If China neglects the practical importance of supporting education in real yuan terms, it won't be too long before its economy begins to feel negative consequences. An often heard argument is that China is still poor and cannot afford to increase its investment in education. But why spend billions of yuan of state money on business banquets? Why so many expensive imported sedan cars for government officials and state business managers? Why so much public money spent for the privileged few to travel for pleasure? Many industrialized nations appropriate an average of 8 percent of their GNP for education, and even a typical Third World country may spend as much as 4 percent. Why not China, a land that used to value scholarship and education so highly, when it now has an economy whose sustained growth depends so much on an educated workforce?

Education holds the key to China's future also in a cultural sense. Why has China proved, since the mid-nineteenth century, so vulnerable in the face of foreign invasions either in the form of gunships or in the form of ideologies or lifestyles? Why did the disastrous 1966–76 Cultural Revolution render a population of over a billion completely defenseless before one man's whims? Why has China's population tripled within less than half a century and created such a burden on its geographic and natural resources? Why, finally, has the thousand-year-old cultural Great Wall come to lie in ruins within a span of just four decades? Poverty is possibly a partial answer to these questions. A more profound answer seems to lie in the weakness of the country's educational system, which failed to produce minds and hearts capable of safeguarding the dignity of humanity and appreciating the sacredness of its culture.

First, China needs an educational system to produce minds and hearts that are capable of feeling confident about themselves in the face of foreign invasions of whatever form. The fact the Marxism, as a foreign ideology, gripped the minds of a billion people for three decades suggests that the Chinese never felt quite confident about their identity. During my recent visits to China, I saw my fellow countrymen drive Lincoln Towncars, wear Rolex watches, smoke Marlboro cigarettes, drink Remy Martin cognac, eat Kentucky Fried chicken, and greet friends with an English "Hello," looking really proud of their new identities in front of their more "earthy" fellow Chinese whom they seem to regard as second-class citizens. Isn't that another sign of cultural weakness? Why, all of a sudden, are the Chinese becoming unsure of themselves again, albeit in a more subtle and indirect way? I guess the answer lies in education, or rather, the lack of education at least on the part of the nouveau riche. *Second, China needs an educational system to produce minds and hearts capable of distinguishing between civilized behaviors and savageries as well as amass the guts to combat savageries.* Had they existed, there wouldn't have been a mass-scale performance of savage behaviors toward fellow citizens and even family members during the Cultural Revolution. *Third, a country as populous as China cannot afford to live in a situation where each and every one of its people goes his or her own direction without a certain level of integration.* "Utter chaos under heaven," which ancient Chinese emperors and Mao had worried about in their lifetimes, can be real and was frequently real in the past two thousand years since the First Emperor of the Qin dynasty. And the most recent example was the 1966–76 Cultural Revolution. This integration, which is cultural and can also be political within certain limits, cannot be realized without the enforcing of a vigorous educational system which should include school, society, and family.

The next question is what needs to be done to effect such an educational system. Or, to use a term that is familiar to China's educators, how should China go about deepening

its educational reforms and establish an educational system
with unique Chinese characteristics?

How to Deepen China's Educational Reforms and Establish an Educational System with Unique Chinese Characteristics?

Based on my experiences as an educator as well as a
student both in China and in Europe and North America, I
believe there are three fundamental issues that need to be
addressed: the hardware issue; the system management
issue; and the software issue. Let me discuss each in turn.

The Hardware Issue

An old Chinese saying goes: "Even a clever housewife
cannot cook a meal without rice." To me, what is even more
important is having a housewife or househusband willing to
cook, without whom no meal will be cooked even if we have
plenty of rice. In our context, teachers are such housewives
and househusbands. How can you possibly find them the
incentive to focus on their teaching responsibilities when they
do not have a livable apartment (I don't even want to use the
word "decent" when speaking about houses in China's urban
cities) and often worry about paying for food? I feel sad to
read stories that accuse schools and teachers of collecting
unjustified fees from students and engaging in nonacademic
activities in order to make some extra money. The worst
thing for a teacher to do is to make money on his or her students, and that's the saddest part of those stories. Here is
one I read about recently. There lived in a rural Chinese village a fisherman who had made good money from his private
fishing business. His mother died and he wanted to show his
fellow villagers that he was a dutiful son. He went to talk to
the principal of a nearby primary school, requesting that he
be allowed to hire a whole class of students to walk and weep
in a funeral procession. The condition for the class to be
excused from school work is to pay the school 200 yuan
(about 25 U.S. dollars) and each participating student five
yuan. "Done deal," the principal said without a question. So

on the day of the funeral, the class, instead of going to school, took part in the walk and cried in order to be paid. Probably it was quite considerate on the part of the principal to create a money-making opportunity for his students since he might feel bad to charge students too many fees each semester. Recently, there have been numerous complaints by the parents of students over being charged dozens of unjustifiable academic fees. Besides tuition, a school can charge a student a miscellaneous fee, an educational fund contribution fee, a lab fee, a school security fee, a school gardening fee, a school maintenance fee, a periodicals fee, a utilities fee, an equipment repair fee, a capital construction fee, a physical education fee, a reading material fee, a class make-up fee, a homework grading fee, an IQ test fee . . . you name it! Are schools to blame? Are teachers to blame? Maybe and maybe not. But why do they do this? Answer: they need money. They need money to survive. Some could not even survive, particularly those who had not, until their very last moment, learned how to take care of themselves. I've heard many stories of how middle-aged professors at universities died in their forties or early fifties due to excessive workload (self-imposed in many cases), malnutrition, and long years of family budgetary pressure. While their students are now scattered all around the country and perhaps the world making their influence on society, big or small, they have ended up lying in graveyards.

It is unfair to claim that the Chinese government and the larger society haven't done anything to help. According to statistics released by the Chinese media, over the past five years, government money or money from various other sources of finance that went into education totaled 320 billion yuan, which was more than double the investment in education over the previous five years. But the problem is that a big portion of the money was eaten up by an excessively redundant administrative and teaching staff. Take China's Beijing University, for example, whicn has a research and teaching faculty of over 2,600, an administrative staff of over 5,000, plus about 2,000 seasonal workers on its payroll. It is a normal practice that the state allocates funds to universities and other school systems based on the size of the research and teaching staff or that of its student population. In the case of Beijing University, the money for the 2,600 faculty size would have to feed an army of almost 10,000!

Despite such problems with "unique Chinese characteristics," China simply doesn't have enough willing "cooking housewives and househusbands" to cook the rice in the academic pot. For example, the School of Journalism of Fudan University in Shanghai had a teaching and research faculty of over fifty when I taught there. In the past few years, many senior professors have retired, more than twenty talented middle-aged and young faculty have come to the United States, and those who remained have been struggling with their own survival (in the pure economic sense). Fudan's journalism program in the old days enjoyed the reputation of being the nation's oldest and best, but where it stands now nobody knows.

What about the "rice" in China's academic cooking pot? The problem is that rice is too much and cooking pots are too few. China would never lack the supply of students, even good students, given the size of its population. No matter how hard the system has been trying to increase its enrollment, there would still be millions of high school graduates well deserving a higher education who would find themselves out of school. There are simply not enough classrooms or qualified teachers for them. Many teenagers can't even go to senior middle school due to space limitations. A phenomenon typical of a publicly or state-owned system is that while there have been calls for more investment, better supply of research equipment and teaching materials, and more classroom space and faculty offices, an enormous amount of resources in universities and various school systems across the country have been or continue to be wasted. This is due to inept management in the educational system.

System Management

Let me start with China's system of higher education. Like other social and organizational systems in the People's Republic, the system of higher education has been managed according to a double-duality management concept, which renders reporting relationships complicated and the functioning of the system inefficient (and hence enormously wasteful of resources as indicated above). The first "duality" is the central government versus the locality, and the second "duality" the party leadership versus the administrative management. The way this double-duality management system is followed varies from university to university. Take Shanghai's Fudan University, for example, which belongs to the category of those under the jurisdiction of the State Commission on Education. Since it gets its funding from Beijing, it is logically subject to the control of the central government in terms of what programs get priority treatment, how many faculty members get promoted to what level, what textbooks should be used, where the students should go after they have graduated (this is being changed), who gets to go abroad as visiting scholars, and so on. Since Fudan University is located in Shanghai, all its nonacademic aspects of life are taken care of by the locality. If a professor, for example, wants to have his or her spouse transferred from another province, he or she would have to go through the Bureau of Personnel of the Shanghai municipal government, which has nothing to do with the State Commission on Education. Most key universities are under the direct control of the central government. The other category is the group of local universities and colleges, which, by definition, belong to the locality. They are funded by the local government which decides, again logically, what programs get approved, who gets promoted, and what kinds of jobs graduating students will be assigned. However, as far as the educational policies are concerned, these lead institutions should also succumb to the control of the central government. This is the first "duality." It is important that the president of a university keep firmly in mind that s/he has two heads looking over his or her shoulder. In the case of technical or professional institutions, funded neither by the State Commission nor by the locality, they would have to report to three "heads": the State Commission on Education for general educational policy advice; the locality for nonacademic affairs; and the ministry from which it receives the money for educational and personnel matters.

The second "duality" is the Party leadership versus the administrative management. Each and every faculty or staff member also has two "heads" to report to within the walls of a university, general or technical, central or local. At the university level, one head is the secretary of the university Party committee, and the other the president. At a lower level, such as the level of a department, one head is the secretary of the Party branch of the department, and the other the academic chairperson. To whom to listen? The Party boss or the administrative boss? You never know. Again take Fudan University, for example. When I was at Fudan, the president was Professor Xie Xide, a well-respected physicist with a Ph.D. from MIT who was also, during her tenure as president of Fudan, a member of the Central Committee of the Chinese Communist Party. The Party boss, at that time, was Mr. Lin Ke, a career Party cadre. I was never quite sure which of the two "heads" had the final say on key university issues. Both of them had my respect together with that of many other faculty and staff members because they proved able to manage the power balance to the extent that life on campus was kept relatively peaceful despite sporadic interferences due to constant political maneuvering by forces either inside or outside the walls of the university. Other campuses may not be that lucky due to the mere fact that there exist two parallel pyramids, the Party hierarchy and the administrative hierarchy, whose constant and often uncompromising and even merciless fight for more influence would leave the campus a chaotic political battleground. There have been calls for "letting the administrative head be in charge" for quite a few years, but no breakthrough has been achieved in the systemic structural reform. Why? Because institutions of higher learning have not yet become places where knowlege is mainly "manufactured"; they still retain many other functions, including, for example, political brainwashing and social policing.

As far as the second "duality" is concerned, primary and middle school education very much follows suit. The dual hierarchies have always existed, and they are still there. The reason for the dual management system is simple: the Party is still the sole leading force in the People's Republic as is stipulated in China's Constitution. Deng Xiaoping's "four insists"—Party leadership; Marxism and Mao Zedong Thought; Socialism; and the People's "democratic dictatorship"—are still valid, at least in theory, which renders a genuine structural reform almost impossible. The Party/ administrative duality exists not only in schools, but in all other organizations. And I believe the system will be there as long as the Party remains the sole leading force and benevolent authoritarianism the political model.

While not much can be done regarding the fundamental political change in the People's Republic (given China's unique circumstances, a more stable political system can better serve the needs of an economic reform than fundamental systemic change, at least for now), a few things can be tried. *First, more autonomy needs to be granted to universities and schools at all levels, wherever they originally belong.* Let them decide by themselves on such matters as how they should allocate funds, who deserves to be promoted or be sent abroad to do research, and what programs should be expanded or cut. Top-down macro-coordination is necessary not only in a planned economy, but also in a market economy. But when it comes to micro management, particularly on issues that are purely academic, government intervention just makes things messy. I can't say how many or what kinds of bureaucratic rules and regulations in the academic area work to delay action or prevent things from happening completely, but I can definitely say with confidence that less government effort to micromanage education would mean better efficiency. *Second, instead of suggesting that the Party leadership and the administrative management be separated, which has been experimented with for many years, I would recommend a "one boss" concept under the condition that benevolent authoritarianism remains the political choice.* Let Party leadership and administrative management reside in one person. Sounds undemocratic? Smacks of authoritarianism? Whatever it is does not matter much as long as it is effective and practical in the sense that it does not conflict with the basic interests of the general populace. Jiang Zemin is the best example: he is concurrently secretary general of the Party and president of the state. If every educational unit follows this example, life for teachers, students, and staff will be much easier. After all, people need only one head looking over their shoulders.

The Software Issue

What to teach at schools and universities? And what kinds of "products" to produce? I have two educational systems in my mind and two sets of teaching experiences to compare: Chinese versus American. It's a challenge that an educator who was basically educated in China ended up teaching in an American university, but I feel I am now in a better position to look at issues of education, including curriculum content. And I wish I could use some of the experiences I have acquired here in American universities as a mirror with which to reflect the issues on the Chinese side. The first issue that comes to my mind is the issue of basic education, that is, education in basic humanities and sciences. To me this represents the foundation of human knowledge and really paves the way for more advanced studies and research. This foundation seems to be weakening not only in China, but also in the United States, and probably in other societies as well. As I moved to teach in other universities in the United States, I gradually accepted the fact that I am in an educational environment that is fast-changing, changing toward a weakened basic education, weakened not only in institutions of higher learning, but also in secondary schools. The Chinese situation might be a little different due to its unique circumstances. Despite their protest, Chinese students, particularly those in primary and middle schools, often find it difficult to loosen themselves up under the watchful eyes of both teachers and parents. However, basic education is also weakening as a result of various kinds of interferences including, for example, a massive exodus of talented teachers into money-making nonacademic professions and jobs, and a limited supply of qualified substitutes. China simply cannot afford to leave the issue unattended to, in universities or in primary and middle schools. Given China's size of population, only a small percentage of senior middle school graduates can expect to enter college; all others have to go to vocational or technical schools or join the workforce. Even though those who will be denied college education and go to work when still young can later benefit from continuing education, their basic education which they received in primary and middle schools will be their main reservoir of acquired knowledge. If you've learned how to write, for example, the skill will be with you for the rest of your life. If, by the time you leave senior middle school, you still have not learned how to read or write, you probably will remain that way for the rest of your life. You can be other-learned, but you can't change the fact that you can't read or write; you're half illiterate.

China has been doing one thing in basic education right. That is the teaching of foreign languages, starting from primary school all the way through graduate school. The present rule is that certain jobs will not be granted to those who have not passed their foreign language test. Foreign languages skills definitely enhance a person's ability to expand his or her knowledge and horizons, to be informed first-hand of the most recent world developments in science and technology, and to help with intercultural and international communication, which is so crucially important in a world that is fast shrinking. I am sure foreign language instruction will continue to be among the priority requirement in all schools and universities in China. Motivation on the part of the students to learn a foreign language, be it English, or Japanese, or German, or French, has never been an issue. They all know the benefits of learning a foreign language, English in particular, because being able to read, speak, and write a popular foreign language means a better chance to go abroad to further one's studies or advance one's career. Indeed, foreign language instruction has been engaging the highest level of enthusiasm on the part of students in basic education, and that pays immensely. The fact that over 40,000 Chinese students are studying in American universities and colleges attests to the great success of the Chinese emphasis on learning English. I myself am a good example of how much one can accomplish with his or her knowledge of English as a second language. I learned to read, speak, and write in English from junior middle school to senior middle school to university to graduate school, all in China. My over-three-decade effort studying the English language as part of my basic education has helped me understand the Melting Pot, communicate my otherwise incommunicable ideas and feelings, conduct some important international scholarly activities, and above all, find a larger world. The American educational system, despite all its advantages (its tremendous resources, for example) and practices that are admirable (such as the institutionalization of system management), seems to be weak in its foreign language programs. In my whole life, I've met with numerous college-educated Americans, and many with advanced degrees—Chinese studies specialists, diplomats, professors, businessmen, travelers, and people from all walks of life, all of whom have a reason to relate to China or Chinese—and I can't remember one or two who were able to communicate, speak or write, in the Chinese language at the professional level. For a Western China specialist to be able to publish in Chinese is a definite rarity. And I always have serious doubts about the China work done by a specialist in Chinese studies who can barely read Chinese. To me, it is an absolute necessity, as the world is edging toward the twenty-first century, for younger generations to be motivated to study and learn one or two foreign languages as part of their basic education. The Chinese system, in this regard, deserves some recognition. And it will prove strategically instrumental in facilitating tremendously the emergence of the Fourth Power.

With basic education on one end of the continuum, the other end is the production of the nation's top minds in science and technology, which seems to be more practically feasible as far as China's resources are concerned. A nation of 1.2 billion people never lacks at least a handful of geniuses in perhaps all scientific and technological fields. And it is always less expensive to "feed" a couple of hundred than to support programs designed to cater to the needs of tens of millions. China in late 1994 released a so-called "hundred-thousand-ten thousand" plan (which definitely smacks of a kind of macro-control by the central government in Beijing) which says that by the year 2,000, China will produce one hundred internationally recognized scientists and scholars (average age 45), one thousand top national academic and research leaders (below age 45), and ten thousand outstanding personnel (aged 30–45) in various disciplines. The *People's Daily* reports that the Chinese Academy of Sciences has decided to put aside 0.2 billion yuan (about 23.5 million U.S. dollars) to help fund the "one hundred's" research and subsidize their housing, with each getting about $235,000.[41] I am not sure if this is the most effective way of turning out scientists and scholars; whether somebody is internationally or nationally recognized does not seem to depend on whether or not the Chinese government wants them to succeed. Their national and international peers will be the judges. It sounds funny to designate "one hundred": no more and no less; "one thousand": no more and no less; and "ten thousand": no more and no less. But as long as it works to produce China's top minds for the twenty-first century, it deserves careful consideration. Never underestimate China's ability to amass its great talents in order to accomplish what it is resolved to accomplish. Remember China successfully tested its first atom bomb in 1964 when the nation was one of the poorest and most backward on earth. The successful explosion of its first atom bomb was a warning to the world that China, as a big, centralized nation, has great power to amass resources— including human talents—to accomplish tasks that small countries cannot hope to accomplish. I believe the "one hundred-one thousand-ten thousand" plan can become reality if the Chinese government is really serious about it. How about the 40,000 Chinese students and scholars many of whom are now emigres to the United States, Japan, Australia, and other countries? If I were to advise the Chinese government on how to handle the relationship with these "drained" brains, I would encourage them to stay put and play the role of bridge-layer instead of asking them to come back home to compete with the "hundred-one thousand-ten thousand" for limited research and living resources. At least for the time being, they will fare better staying where they are than returning home to serve, even from the Chinese government's perspective. Having 40,000 Chinese minds study and work in America's top universities, national research labs, and Fortune 500 companies will be strategically beneficial to China as well as to the United States.

The Chinese government seems to be ambivalent toward this brain drain to more competitive systems. It's a love-hate relationship. Those students and scholars who had supported their colleagues in Tiananmen in June of 1989 have generally been pardoned and are allowed to return. But what if they become active again once they are back in China? What if they bring in liberal ideas to stir up new trouble on Chinese campuses? I am not sure if these are practically valid questions any longer; the university campus culture has changed greatly since the bloody ending of the Tiananmen tragedy. It's now more cynical than politically enthusiastic and naive, more practical than idealistic, more obsessed with pleasure-seeking than hardworking, and more concerned about whether or not economically rewarding jobs follow graduation than about human dignity. The Chinese, including the Chinese students, are a very forgetful people; Tiananmen seems to look remotely distant and becomes quite irrelevant to their life. What does all this mean?

It means that something more needs to be said about the "software issue" of China's educational system. I am never quite for any movement or activity designed to disrupt the political and social stability of the 1.2 billion people whose preoccupation is the nation's economic development. With all stakes of its economic reforms on the line, China cannot afford to have "utter chaos under heaven." However, I also believe schools and universities to be places where it should be encouraged to "let one hundred schools of thought contend," as Mao said over three decades ago. To me, schools and universities are market places for ideas, all kinds of ideas including Marxist and non-Marxist ideas. The Party has the right to declare Marxism and Mao Zedong Thought to be the guiding ideology for its members, but it should also let other ideologies, to use Mao's word, "contend," as long as those who advocate alternative ideologies do not intend to incite violence to disrupt social stability. When Mao said "let one hundred schools of thought contend," he must have included non-Marxist schools of thought among the "one hundred." It's too long that this policy of Mao's has been left unattended to. It's too long that students and teachers in the People's Republic have been deprived of their right to freedom of speech. And it's too long that academic conscience for truth has been suppressed.

As ideologies, Marxism and Maoism have their right to exist, not only in Chinese schools and universities, but everywhere. But one man's ideology, no matter how powerful, is, after all, one man's ideology. And no man is God. No human violence is more immoral than the imposition of one man's ideology on a whole people. I still remember those Friday afternoon study sessions where faculty and staff gathered to study Chairman Mao's works and conducted criticism and self-criticism. Students would hold separate study meetings. Such political study sessions were instrumental in politicizing campus life and worked to suffocate free thinking and free speech.

It's very unfortunate that there has always been fear on the part of those in power that free expression of ideas could weaken the ideological leadership of the Party, which could eventually lead to "utter chaos under the heaven." This was very much unproved in China's history: each revolution and uprising in recorded Chinese history, that is, the overthrow of one class by another, was always triggered by nonideological events. Even the Tiananmen tragedy, often thought of as the result of the liberalization of ideas, was indeed an inevitable response to the alleged corruption charges against the Party and government officials. I think it is time to call for an emancipation of ideologies from the yoke of the "Friday afternoon" mind-set. Let scholars speak their mind and heart. Let them no longer write with a trembling hand. Let as many schools of thought contend as possible. A free market of goods must go hand in hand with a relatively free market of ideas.

I am not here to advocate absolute freedom of speech. There exists, nowhere in the world, either an absolute free market of goods or an absolute free market of ideas. *Freedom goes together with responsibility, responsibility is tied to discipline, and effective discipline is based on moral values.* Education as a process, to me, is more than creating and transmitting knowledge or ideas. It is how culturally acceptable morals and behaviors get to be passed down from generation to generation. Is teaching values part of the task of schools and universities? The issue seems more complicated in the United States than in China, since the former is more multicultural than the latter. While I will not comment on this issue for the American educational system, I am strongly of the position that teaching values should be part of the task of Chinese schools and universities. And I want to emphasize the importance of teaching traditional Chinese values to younger generations.

China is unique in that the forces of modernization have been compounded by those of revolution that have affected or even altered the very nature of its traditional value system. Such influences started as early as the mid-nineteenth century when China's door was forced open by the Opium War with Britain and continued through the early twentieth century. The May 4th Movement of 1919[42] raged through Chinese university campuses amidst such slogans as "Down with Confucianism." The Cultural Revolution of 1966–76 later proved to be much more radical and destructive in bombarding traditional cultural values. The economic reforms Deng launched in late 1978 or early 1979 have brought mixed results in terms of restoring traditional values: some were revived and others were distorted to accommodate Western value orientations. In the China survey Godwin Chu and I did, we presented our respondents with eighteen traditional values and asked them to tell us which ones they felt proud of, which ones they wanted to discard, and which ones they had no opinion about. Based on the responses we received from a 2,000-subject sample, we were able to construct an index of endorsement (the percentage of those who said feeling proud minus the percentage of those who wanted to discard) for each of the 18 values:

Long historical heritage	89.7
Diligence and frugality	86.2
Loyalty and devotion to state	67.5
Benevolent father, filial son	48.0
Generosity and virtues	39.8
Respect for traditions	38.5
Submission to authority	33.2
Harmony is precious	29.5
Tolerance, propriety, deference	25.3
Chastity for women	–13.5
Glory to ancestors	–23.8
A house full of sons and daughters	–35.5
Farmers high, merchants low	–43.3
Pleasing superiors	–48.9
Discretion for self-preservation	–55.9
Differentiation between men and women	–59.2
Way of golden mean	–59.6
Three obediences and four virtues	–64.0

What's interesting is that the eighteen traditional values were evenly divided with nine receiving positive endorsement and nine negative evaluation. Such values as "three obediences and four virtues"[43] undoubtedly deserved to be discarded. But I am not sure whether "way of golden mean"[44] and even "discretion for self-preservation" should be rated that low. What was shocking to us was the fact that the value of "way of golden mean," which used to be one of the most important traditional values in China, received the strongest negative opinion after "three obediences and four virtues." "Way of golden mean," when treated as a theory of revolution or an economic theory, will collide head-on with Marxist–Leninist–Mao Zedong Thought on the one hand and capitalistic greed for profit on the other. All Communist revolutionaries in China including the late Chairman Mao and the late essayist Lu Xun attacked it vehemently. But the "way of golden mean," viewed as a philosophy of life advocating not going to extremes, functions to harmonize human relationships and pacify human souls. To prevent society from becoming physically violent and ideologically polarized, and to prevent individuals from becoming excessively greedy, we need a little of the "way of golden mean," and we need to educate students in schools and universities in this value.

The "way of golden mean" is only one example. There are other values that are worth reinforcing. Schools and universities can highlight one or two or more traditional values and make them part of their organizational value system; it is never realistically possible to educate students with a so-called refined, socially acceptable value system, which indeed is in its own process of formation or reformation due to constant social change. The whole point is that schools and universities should take as part of their mission the teaching of values. It is instrumentally important for a nation of 1.2 billion to have a certain level of integration. Nowadays, diversity is a popular word, but integration is equally important, probably more so for China than for any other society under the present circumstances.

7

The Chinese Family: The Most Sustainable Resource of the Fourth Power

For thousands of years, close family relations have been a major cornerstone of traditional Chinese culture.

—Chu and Ju, *The Great Wall in Ruins*

Family: *The* Place Chinese Want to Be

As I have mentioned quite a few times in the previous chapters, Godwin Chu, a senior researcher at the East-West Center in Hawaii, and I conducted a major cultural survey in the People's Republic of China in 1989, the findings of which were reported in our co-authored book *The Great Wall in Ruins: Communication and Cultural Change in China.* We wanted to know, while we were designing our survey questionnaire, to what extent the 1966–76 Cultural Revolution had affected Chinese culture and China's social institutions including the Chinese family. The overall damage was found to be widespread and fundamental, hence our title *The Great Wall in Ruins.* But we were surprised to have found the Chinese family, like a rock standing on the shore of an ocean, having survived the crushing waves of numerous social revolutions including the most recent, the Cultural Revolution. The values of family were still solidly there, and family relations remained close. As we indicated in our book:

One of the most significant findings . . . is that the family, a cornerstone of Chinese culture, has survived the turmoils of the Cultural Revolution. During the height of the

Cultural Revolution, children were incited to denounce their parents. Husbands and wives accused each other for their own survival. For a time, when Mao's struggle theory went into full play, fears spread across the country that traditional Chinese family relations, which had been valued for thousands of years, would finally fall apart. Such fears proved to be unfounded. The chaotic effects of these ten destructive years proved to be transitory. The Cultural Revolution failed to remove the soil in which Chinese family had been planted.[45]

Such soil is even more fertile in Taiwan. A similar survey was later conducted in Taiwan, and parts of the findings were used to compare with the mainland Chinese data in a recently published book entitled *To See Ourselves: Comparing Traditional Chinese and American Cultural Values*.[46] We have heard numerous stories about successful Chinese family businesses in Taiwan, Hong Kong, Singapore, and other Southeast Asian countries such as Thailand, Malaysia, Indonesia, and the Philippines. It is not an exaggeration to say that the Chinese family remains a stronghold of traditional Chinese culture wherever there are Chinese, in China or elsewhere in the world, notwithstanding the fact that the Chinese revolution of 1949 had very much removed the economic base of the age-old clan system on the mainland. The values had been so deeply rooted in an average Chinese person's psychology and behavior that the soil had all along refused to be removed even though what was above the soil might have been partially or even wholly damaged. Our scientific surveys have proved so, and my own life experiences have definitely convinced me over and over again that anything can be sacrificed—professional or political career, personal property, individual freedom, and even love—but not your family. To me, family is what has prevented Chinese culture from falling apart through numerous social upheavals, and familism is that which defines Chineseness. There can be identified hundreds of cultural values and behavioral patterns in Chinese culture, but the ones regarding family have always been the primary, the most sacred, and all others are secondary or tertiary or even expendable when one's family is at stake. I love to tell the following story and like to use it as an example to prove that some cultural practices which uphold the integrity of family may sound ridiculously excessive to a Western ear: Once upon a time, a proud prince of a feudal kingdom told Confucius: "In my country there is an upright man. When his father stole a sheep, he bore witness against him." Confucius said: "The upright men in my community are different from this. The father conceals the misconduct of the son and the son the misconduct of the father. Uprightness is thus defined."[47] This is indeed a story about how filial piety or familial loyalty should be upheld. As we know, filial piety has been the root of all virtues in Confucianism. Confucius believed that the primary moral duty of filial piety must be upheld even at the expense of other moral obligations. Whoever violates this primary moral duty may be regarded at the least an immoral son or daughter, even in today's China. There were quite a few such cases, during the 1966–76 Cultural Revolution, where a son or daughter was forced by Red Guards to stand up and make public accusations against his or her father or mother's counterrevolutionary activities. A young writer in 1978 published a short story that tells of the agony and remorse experienced by a senior middle school girl in Shanghai who had denounced her mother and then volunteered to leave home for a remote village to receive ideological reform. When she returned to Shanghai after the Cultural Revolution, she wanted to tell her mother how much she regretted her betrayal and to beg forgiveness. All was too late. Her health ruined by torture during the Cultural Revolution, Mother had died the day before. The story became an immediate hit, and the young writer, who was then studying in Shanghai's Fudan University during my tenure there, rose to the status of a celebrity. It was the theme of the story—agony and remorse over familial betrayal—that touched the hearts of millions of readers. The story, called *The Scars*, soon led to a new wave of novels and stories known as the "scars literature," an important entry in the history of Chinese contemporary literature. Betrayals, including familial betrayals, are a common social phenomenon in all cultures including Chinese culture. But I have no doubt that in all Chinese history, familial betrayals have been depicted as an utter sin. Even though there were all kinds of stories telling of familial betrayals during the Cultural Revolution—where the betrayers were hailed by the Gang-of-Four[48] controlled media as revolutionary heroes and heroines—many of such betrayals were mere strategies carefully designed between, for example, a son accuser and a father accused, in order to save both from getting into further trouble. I personally participated in and witnessed the whole Cultural Revolution; it was a revolution where no one had a place to flee except one's family. One's home might be searched any time at the will of Red Guard hooligans in the name of making revolution, but not your family. One's loved ones—parents, children, or spouse— might be sent afar to receive labor reform, but not their hearts and hopes. During the whole ten-year period, every Chinese learned to tell lies in public, to tell how loyal they were to Chairman Mao and how much they wanted to be part of the revolution. There was only one place where they could speak their hearts, share true emotions, and talk out their frustrations, the place where they felt safe and warm and willing to cry. That was at home with one's parents or children or spouse. I have a theory that mainland Chinese familial relations, at least among nuclear families, may have become closer due to the sanctuary role they played during the ten darkest years between 1966 and 1976 in China's history. It was the Chinese family that had prevented China from falling apart and the cultural Great Wall from becoming completely ruined. And it is my guess that the Chinese family will play an essential role in reviving a very much disintegrated culture and a weak value and belief system.

One has to be very careful when "collectivism" or even "communalism" is used to describe the core value of Chinese culture. I see collectivism or communalism as an extension of familism. Without a good understanding of where collectivism or communalism came from, one may assume that an average Chinese would always try to put the interests of a group above his or her personal interests. One has to seriously ask what this "group" is. Is it an ingroup or an outgroup? Even if it is an ingroup, it may not be as "in" as one that is composed of family members. Groups, like other social systems, are also hierarchically ordered. The closer a group is to a person's family, the more importance he or she will attach to that group. It's like throwing a stone into a pond, sending ripples toward the periphery. The farther the ripple from where the stone was dropped, the less it would matter to the center. The family is where the center is. It won't be too much of a risk to assume that an average Chinese wouldn't care too much about a group of strangers under normal circumstances, but it would be an entirely different story if his or her family interests are on the line. To capture the accuracy of a concept used to describe the core value of Chinese culture, I would recommend familism to replace collectivism or communalism; to me the latter two are a mere extension or transformation of the former.

I also want to argue that the family as the center of the cultural universe is going to be the most sustainable force of the Fourth Power. Today's business environment, as national and regional economies are becoming increasingly globalized, changes faster, or much faster, than in any previous historical period. Nothing seems to hold still any more, and everything is moving so fast that it is getting increasingly difficult, if not yet impossible, to identify structures. The fancy word is process, no longer structure; structure suggests stability, or status quo in a bad sense. Rapid technological, economic, and political changes, plus fundamental social and values changes, have sent the whole world, both the West and East, into bewilderment, feeling unprepared for this chaos. Some people love talking about how politically unstable, economically chaotic, and culturally immoral Chinese society is, and how hopeless its future will be since the culture will be quite unable to meet the challenges of the magnitude of worldly changes. They often forget one thing: Chinese families—their cohesiveness, unity, spirit of sacrifice, discipline, and ever-present resolve to survive and live or at least hope to live a bit better. While such familial values are fast weakening or diminishing in some cultures, they are consolidating and refuse to die in Chinese families on the mainland, and in Taiwan, Hong Kong, and other parts of the world. Like any other social system in any other society, Chinese family cannot simply escape the influence of a fast-changing world. Nevertheless, it doesn't look like it's ready to give up in the face of a structurally and morally changed world. Many of the family-related values are still solidly there.

An Analysis of Family-Related Values

Among the most sustainable resources for China and the Fourth Power is a system of family-related values. Each and every one of them is important not only for maintaining the life of Chinese family but also can be instrumental for revitalizing organizations and the larger society. To facilitate this analysis, I will see family as a mini–social hierarchy, a communication system, and a basic unit of production, each of which is based on a set of family-related values.

Family as a Mini–Social Hierarchy

From a structural point of view, Chinese family is a mini–social hierarchy. Millions of such mini–social hierarchies combine to form the larger social hierarchy of Chinese society. Indeed the hierarchical nature of Chinese society is very much mirrored in familial values endorsing family as a social hierarchy. Such values include filial piety, respect and deference, loyalty, benevolence, responsibility, and discipline, all of which may be grouped into two subcategories: values pertaining to an ascending order and values supporting a descending mandate. Let me analyze each of them.

Filial piety, respect and deference, and loyalty combine to endorse an ascending familial order.

Filial piety. This is one of the core familial values in Chinese culture, the most important and unviolable. It's utter sin for a son or daughter not to cherish a lifelong, unreserved devotion and obligation to his or her parents. *The Twenty-four Stories of Filial Piety*, which children were required to read and study as part of their early education in traditional China, contains many such illustrations. In one story, a young boy was worried that mosquitoes might be disturbing his father. So every night during the summer, before his father went to sleep, he would lie in his bed and let the mosquitoes feed on him until they were so full that they would not bite his father. In another story, the mother wanted to eat fish on an icy winter day. The dutiful son unrobed himself and lay on a frozen pond until the ice melted to enable him to catch a fish for his mother. In one of the Chinese classic novels, *The Dream of the Red Chamber*, the hero's grandmother is depicted as the matriarch in the Jia family, for whom devotion is an absolute, unchallengeable daily ritual. When Baoyu, the hero, receives a spanking from his father due to his failure to focus on his studies or for some other reason, the only person that can save him is his grandmother. The moment she appears, the hero's father, who is doing the spanking, would kneel down and beg his mother's forgiveness. This is filial piety in Chinese interpretation. During the Cultural Revolution, in order to fan popular worship of Chairman Mao, there was designed a slogan that read "Dear is Father, and dear is Mother, but the dearest is Chairman Mao" which was extremely effective in transforming a traditional value into an instrument that served the goal of politics. What was contained in the slogan was the notion that one's utmost devotion should be reserved for Chairman Mao since he was even dearer than one's parents, to whom devotion had been unquestionably obligatory all through China's civilization.

Respect and deference. Respect for parents is always coupled with a feeling of deference. When I write to my mother, for example, I refrain from calling her "Dear Mother," which would suggest intimacy, but not enough deference. Instead, I write "Mother the Great" (*muqin daren*) to begin my letter. Legend has it that traditional Chinese rites and proprieties originated from seating arrangements in ancient times. The places of honor at a square table would each face south and would always be reserved for parents at home. The value of respect and deference is a moral one, more than a mere mannerism. *It is a widely shared belief among the Chinese that if one doesn't even know how to respect one's parents with deference, all his talk of respect or politeness is hypocritically shallow.* A son or daughter, in today's society as well as in traditional Chinese culture, is supposed to consult his or her parents on various personal matters, big or small, not necessarily because his or her parents have more wisdom or experience or are more trustworthy, but because they deserve respect and reference. In other words, merely asking one's parents for their opinion should be viewed as a cultural ritual with which to reinforce the moral value of respect and deference. In our China survey, we asked this question: "Do your children consult you on their problems?"[49] An overwhelming 90.2 percent of our respondents who had children said they did either often or sometimes. In traditional Chinese culture, children were not allowed to object to their parents' decisions, opinions, or even suggestions, which were often interpreted as "orders" the children must obey. Today, parents' words may not carry the weight of "orders," but they must be treated seriously. We also asked in our survey: "Generally speaking, when you ask your children to do something, do they talk back?"[50] One-third of our respondents (33.9 percent) said their children hardly ever talked back when asked to do something. Half of them (51.1 percent) said sometimes they did. Only a small percentage (15.0 percent) complained that their children talked back under most circumstances. Our survey findings clearly suggest that the value of respect and reference on the part of children still permeates Chinese families.

Loyalty. In a hierarchically ordered, familial culture, children are not regarded as independent human entities; rather they are an extension of their parents' soul and flesh. Therefore, complete loyalty to parents is socially expected of their children. In the Confucian story I told earlier, in order to be an "upright man," the son was not supposed to bear witness against his father's stealing of the sheep. In other words, the son would become an "upright man" if he remained loyal to his father (and, of course, vice versa) even to the extent that secondary moral obligations might be violated. *The Scars* story touched the hearts of millions of Chinese in the late 1970s because of the popular appeal of its theme—a daughter's remorse over the betrayal of her mother. In *Farewell, My Concubine*, a 1993 winner of the Cannes International Film Festival, the hero betrayed his lover out of fear of his own persecution by the Cultural Revolution. Tragic as it is, such betrayal may not be as tragic as parental betrayal in the eyes of an average Chinese; loyalty to one's parents is absolutely unquestionable.

To match the three ascending hierarchical familial values, there are three values that endorse a descending relationship at home. These are the values of benevolence, responsibility, and discipline. Let me explain each briefly.

Benevolence. Called *ren* in Chinese, benevolence is the most important concept in Confucian humanism, for it covers all human relationships including familial relationships. Indeed, *ren* is the very core of Confucian moral virtues. Practicing benevolence starts from within the family, the parental relationship in particular. Confucius says: "Few of those who are filial and respectful brothers will show disrespect to superiors, and there has never been a man who is respectful to superiors and yet creates disorder." "Filial piety and brotherly respect are the root of *ren*." Who planted this "root" in the family? The answer is the parents. One of the eighteen traditional Chinese values Godwin Chu and I studied, which I mentioned earlier, was "benevolent father, filial son." In traditional Chinese culture a "benevolent father" was one who was supposed to do everything possible to get his son a good education so that he could have a successful future and stay filial. The classical *Three-Character Scripture* in traditional China writes: "If a son is uneducated, the father is to blame." In our China survey, we found that a majority of our respondents (60.8 percent) still felt proud of the value of "benevolent father, filial son." And I have no problem believing that this value is even more strongly held in Taiwan and Hong Kong.

Responsibility. Good Chinese parents are said to have to fulfill three major responsibilities towards their children: to obtain them a good education, a good job, and a good wife or husband. The findings of our China survey have attested to all of them. Traditional China was a society of very limited career opportunities. By the time most Chinese entered the workforce, their life was pretty much fixed. Some Chinese, particularly those of the Buddhist faith, practiced merit-making so that their next life would be better. Most Chinese parents pinned their hopes on their children and would do whatever they could to support their children's education. They saw this as a responsibility they were most willing to fulfill in the past, and they are very much that way today. However, Chinese parents are not yet happy when their children have got a good education and a good job; they also want to see to it that their children marry well. Godwin Chu and I asked two questions which would have little chance of being included in a typical Western social survey: "If you have a daughter, and she carries on with several boyfriends before she gets married, what would you think about this?" "If you have a son, and he carries on with several girlfriends before he gets married, what would you think about this?" The response patterns were nearly identical for daughters and sons. An overwhelming majority, 72.9 percent for daughters and 72.1 percent for sons, would not permit such behavior. This may be called "unwanted interference" in the West. The Chinese parents see it as a kind of parental responsibility.

Discipline. Again, I want to use some of the findings of our China survey to support the belief that disciplining of children as a value is still held as important in today's China. We asked the question: "In child rearing, which is more important, to let children develop freely as much as possible, or to teach them to follow rules?" Not to our surprise, nearly two-thirds of the respondents (64.2 percent) considered it more important to teach children to follow rules. Traditionally, Chinese parents believed in strict punishment as a way of disciplining children. Spanking was a common practice. As a popular Chinese saying goes, "Use the rod unsparingly, and you will have dutiful children." We asked: "At what age do you think it is inappropriate to spank your children?" The way we phrased the question implied that spanking was acceptable, so that our respondents would be more willing to answer truthfully. As it turned out, only about one in nine said children should not be spanked at all. Most said spanking as a way of disciplining children was necessary: 20.4 percent said spanking could continue until children reached 3–4 years old; 12.4 percent said it would remain appropriate until children reached 5–6 years old; 18.6 percent said until 7–8 years old; 10 percent said until 9–10 years old; 6.8 percent said until 11–12 years old; 7.7 percent said until 13–14 years old; 7.4% said until 15–16 years old. And there were 5.5 percent who said parents could continue spanking their children until they reached 17–18 years old. It should be noted that some 20 percent of our respondents considered spanking children an appropriate punishment until they became teenagers. Attitudes toward spanking were quite uniform among most of our respondents. We found no differences in terms of age, gender, or education as a relevant factor.

Family as a Communication System

The hierarchical nature of familial relationships, particularly those between parents and children, dictates the way the family communication is conducted, both verbally and nonverbally. If the issue is looked at from a reversed angle, I would suggest that it is through communication that hierarchically ordered familial relationships are realized and regulated. It is inconceivable that there exists, for example, a father-son relationship where the father doesn't, using whatever symbolic means, communicate his love and responsibility to the son and the son never communicates his respect and reference to the father. In chapter 3, I discussed social positioning and role communication as that which reinforces social hierarchy and regulates social/business resources. If we expand the notion of communication to refer to any symbolic action which realizes and regulates social relationships including familial relationships, then both social positioning and role communication belong to the larger category of human communication.

What is important to know is that social positioning and role communication in Chinese society begins within the family, where the purest form of social positioning and role communication can be identified. Parents and children, elder brother and younger brother, elder sister and younger sister are never confused about each other's position in the family, and each familial role is asserted and celebrated through the practice of such communication rituals as use of honorific (particularly when one writes to his or her parents), seating arrangements, body language, and speaking opportunities (e.g., when parents are talking with guests, children are not allowed to cut in to make comments unless they are asked). *Familial communication in traditional Chinese culture was strictly based on the differentiation of role identities in terms of who was at the top, who was on the bottom, and who was in the middle.* There have been some changes as far as the limitations of children's freedoms are concerned, but it is still very much the case, as far as my own experiences can tell, that a person's "I" identity tends to be suppressed. It is not just that children's individuality needs to be suppressed when they are at home; parents do the same, just as Confucius says, "behave like a father when you are being a father, and behave like a son when you are being a son." I don't know to what extent Chinese are a less humorous people than Americans or Europeans, but I have no doubt that there has never been much humor in a typical Chinese family. All family members are too serious performing their roles to go beyond the line, even occasionally, to show his or her talent at joke-making.

The value of role communication is rooted in Confucian *li*, or rules of proprieties which have been governing human relationships for the past 2,000 years in China, despite the fact *li* has been added to, deducted from, and modified during different dynasties and historical periods including that of the People's Republic. Of course, Confucian *li* was vehemently attacked and the practicing of it considered anti-revolutionary during the 1966–76 Cultural Revolution. What was interesting, however, was that a new set of "revolutionary" *li* rules or proprieties governing revolutionary relationships were so similar in form to Confucian *li*. In the ten-year chaos, no matter how chaotic society could become with different factions fighting against each other verbally or physically, the Mao- and Party-dominated hierarchy was always crystal-clear: no one could afford to be confused about who was at the absolute top and therefore unchallengeable, who was above the Central Committee of the Party, who was below the Central Committee, and so on. At the absolute top and unchallengeable was, of course, Chairman Mao, to whom loyalty was enforced through a set of communication rituals that were reserved for him alone. For example, these words were all reserved for Mao: "the great leader, great comman-der-in-chief, great teacher, and great helmsman." Whoever claimed to deserve to be called such, intentionally or care-lessly, must die. This was indeed what actually happened during the height of the madness: Whoever shouted "Down with Mao," must die. Whoever tore up a portrait of Mao, must die. Whoever dared to curse Mao with a four-letter word, must die ten thousand times. This was part of the "revolu-tionary order": a Party Central Committee member would have to listen to a Politburo member; a Politburo member would have to listen to a standing Politburo member; a standing Politburo member would have to listen to Jiang Qin, Mao's wife; and, of course, all would have to listen to Mao. One of the most important leadership skills for those cadres that had political ambitions was how to use communications to show his or her superior in the political hierarchy his or her knowledge and appreciation of the differentiation between the role he or she was playing and the role that his or her superior was playing. Those who failed to demonstrate that knowledge or appreciation might soon lose his or her favor or even precious life under some extraordinary circum-stances. That was the price one must be ready to pay for any violation of revolutionary *li*.

Confucian *li* gradually resurfaced as ultra-leftist revolu-tionary *li* became outdated or were discarded. Once again, it's okay to pay tribute to one's ancestors within an extended family by performing such communication rituals as burning incense or paper money. Within the nuclear family, however, Confucian *li* regarding familial relationships were indeed always practiced even during the most difficult years—the first few years—of the Cultural Revolution when revolutionary *li* were followed in public.

Family as a Production Unit

Family has always been a production unit for thousands of years in rural China except during the time when rural production was collectivized under the People's Commune system that began in 1958. The commune system was abolished in 1982, and since then China's rural productivity has significantly increased, paving the way for urban reform. In urban China, the role of family as a production unit—if "production" means that of material goods—was, starting from mid-nineteenth century, gradually taken over by organizations and businesses for which urban residents were hired to do a job and receive a salary or wage. But whether in rural China or urban China, the Chinese family as a production unit in the larger sense of the word "production" has always been the case; Chinese families have always been willing and ready to "do a good job" at "producing" a next generation. Therefore, production is both production of material goods and production of people. The Chinese are a people proven to succeed at both.

The Chinese have learned the value of hardwork, savings, division of labor, and investment in education from the very experience of managing family as a production unit. I will discuss two important values relating to family as a production unit: the value of hard work and that of savings.

The value of hard work. I never quite understood why hard work should be so important to the Chinese until I had traveled around the world and had seen with my own eyes the difference between fertile land and barren soil, between a rich country and a poor country, and between hard work and laziness. China, with its 9,600 million square kilometers of yellow earth tilled for thousands of years, feeds 1.2 billion people, one-fifth of the world's population. Even if it had rich and abundant natural resources, which is unfortunately not the case with China, a people of this size would have to work very hard merely to survive. China's recorded history seems to have proven one thing: since ancient times, nature has not been friendly to the people living in China—there have been numerous floods, droughts, and famines. There was only one thing over which the Chinese had full control: a pair of diligent hands.

The value of hard work, which has always been associated with family as a production unit, is still esteemed by the Chinese. The progress and development we have seen in rural China since 1982, the year of the abolition of the commune system, have been phenomenal. I have a couple of relatives living in the suburbs of Shanghai. They could barely feed themselves during the People's Commune in the sixties and seventies because all their incentives to produce were killed by the system. But as soon as the land was redistributed to them, they became the hardest-working people on earth. The world around them changed almost overnight. And they soon became "rich," compared with what they had had before. Now all of them have built brandnew two-storey houses! "How could you manage it?," I asked when I was visiting them in the summer of 1994. They showed me their hands and said "by working hard."

Many of the Chinese immigrants from mainland China now living in the United States had nothing but a head between two shoulders plus a suitcase when they first arrived. But the family hung on together, with each member working two or three jobs and earning $3–5 an hour. They had no cars, no medical insurance, no vacations, no holidays, no movies, no music, no dining-out, and, of course, many of them had no English. All they had were two hands and a willingness to use them. They worked under the harshest conditions that one could ever imagine, but they were quiet and content. Many of them simply became living working machines! But finally their hard work paid off: in less than ten years, many of them own a small family business, a home, and possibly two cars. But still no vacations, no holidays, no dining-out, no "unnecessary" spending. They continue to work hard, and continue to save.

The value of saving. Saving makes one feel secure financially, particularly when one lives in an unfriendly natural environment of limited resources and doesn't know what may happen in the future. Saving makes it possible for a small family business to expand and reproduce, and it's less costly than taking a loan. Saving can help realize one's dream of living a better life. Most importantly, saving can accumulate enough funds to send children to better schools to give them a better education. I've mentioned in the previous paragraph that my relatives living in the suburbs of Shanghai were able to build new houses, and many mainland Chinese immigrants now living in the United States have turned their economic status around from having nothing to owning a small family business together with a home. Mere hard work wasn't enough to make this happen; saving has definitely been instrumental. Imagine this: if each and every one of the 1.2 billion population saves just one dollar a year and puts it in the Bank of China, how much money will the Bank of China collect? An easy 1.2 billion dollars! What financial strength can China muster with the nation's saving rate staying around 30–35 percent?

I have briefly discussed nine traditional values relating to the Chinese family as a mini-hierarchy, as a communication system, and as a production unit. These are the values of filial piety, respect and deference, loyalty, benevolence, responsibility, discipline, *li*-based role communication, hard work, and saving. I may sound like I'm preaching these values, though I am not. I do not believe that familism is better than individualism regardless of the circumstances, or vice versa. Familism may not prove to be productive or even morally acceptable in the United States, and individualism can hardly be appreciated in the eyes of Chinese familists. But I do believe, however, that the nine traditional values can be transformed to serve at least some instrumental goals of China and the Fourth Power.

Transformation of Familial Values

Let me list again the nine values I discussed above:

1. Filial piety
2. Respect and reference
3. Loyalty
4. Benevolence
5. Responsibility
6. Discipline
7. *Li*-based role communication
8. Hard work
9. Saving

Let's see to what extent these traditional family-originated values can help in modern businesses and organizations and in the larger society. I will discuss how Chinese organizations, either government-controlled or privately owned, will function as a mini-hierarchy, a communication system, and a production unit with the above-listed nine values transformed to serve their instrumental purposes.

Chinese organizations, like families, are also invariably mini-hierarchies which combine to form with other social systems the hierarchically ordered Chinese society. Whether a business is controlled by the state or owned by private individuals does not make a difference in terms of the hierarchical nature of its structure. It may well be the case that a government-controlled organization can even be more hierarchical than a private business, and vice versa. Any structure that is hierarchical brings with it the issue of how power is shared, and it's often an absolute requirement that authority be respected in order to assure an orderly organizational life. The Chinese, because of their nurturing in a family environment where they learned to respect and appreciate authority, seem to draw immense psychological gratification from worshipping authority, somebody above them with some power to wield. They will continue to worship authority unless authority has been abused so much that its very survival is being threatened. All three ascending values relating to familial hierarchy—filial piety, respect and reference, and loyalty—fit well with organizational hierarchies. Indeed, the majority of Chinese organizations irrespective of location, whether on the mainland, or in Taiwan, or in Hong Kong, or in other parts of the world, would expect all organization members to be respectful of and loyal to the ownership and management. Challenge in any form could be read as offensive or even subversive, resulting in a strain on the management-labor relationship at best and termination of employment at worst.

Looking at the hierarchy from the top, the ownership and management of an organization are expected to take good care of their employees, just like parents take good care of their children. Therefore, the transformed version of the three descending familial values of benevolence, responsibility, and discipline becomes as important to the ownership and management just as the transformed version of filial piety, respect and deference, and loyalty is to the organization members. Take my former employer, Fudan University of Shanghai, for example. My whole life was dependent on it: the system would have to give me an apartment to live; it would have to arrange for me to go to a good hospital if I fell ill; it would have to help find a good school for my child; it would have to send staff over to help if there was a burglary around my apartment building; and so on. And, like all my colleagues, I expected it to do all that. The first "cultural shock" I experienced the moment I arrived at the university that hired me here in the United States was that they did not have an apartment ready for me to live in! Later I realized that such matters would be the responsibility of employees themselves; colleagues could help, but the employer wouldn't bother setting up "an employees housing department."

There is no doubt that an organization, like a family, is a communication system. Role communication, as I defined in chapter 3, is a process in which interactants use communication to emphasize each other's role identity. "I" identity tends to be suppressed in the interaction. While role communication, if not used skilfully, might dampen an organization member's creativity, it nevertheless helps maintain an orderly and predictable organizational life. Effective role communication depends on organization members' reasonably good understanding of each other's role in an organization. Such reasonably good understanding is very much based on years or maybe decades of experience in interacting with each other. That means that one member knows another person and his or her role so well that the mere utterance of one or two Chinese characters may be more than sufficient to accomplish what could not be done without an exchange of ten documents. In other words, role communication in a Chinese organization always overlaps with interpersonal interaction. It's like communication between a father and a son: no matter how long they've lived together and how well they know each other, the father keeps talking like a father and the son keeps talking like a son—neither is supposed to be confused about his set role. One of the primary goals of practicing Confucian li-based role communication is to help maintain existing social relationships. Therefore, one of the primary goals of practicing role communication in organizations is, understandably, to maintain the existing, hierarchically ordered organizational relationships. Since an organizational hierarchy is defined not only in terms of how much authority and power one has in a particular organization but also in terms of his or her seniority of employment, professional rank, perceived qualifications, work experience, age, and even political affiliation (as far as mainland Chinese organizations are concerned), role communication must be conducted in such a way that such "hierarchical elements" are respected and upheld. In other words, a hierarchical order exists horizontally as well as vertically, and both vertical and horizontal hierarchies must be maintained using role communication in order to assure a peaceful working milieu, with each member being keenly aware of where he or she should stand.

Being a production unit, whether profit-oriented or nonprofit, no organization can function well without hardworking members and a solid financial backing. Here is introduced the possibility of transforming the values of hard work and saving relating to the family as a production unit into an organizational setting. Small Chinese family businesses are the best examples with which to prove the importance of hard work and the spirit of saving, which have been instrumental in bringing so many mom and pop businesses to the grand stage of entrepreneurial success. Organizations need more than hard-working employees and a sufficient cash flow to succeed; they also need leadership, teamwork, good personnel policies, technologies, planning, marketing, and public relations. But hard work and the spirit of saving are among the most basic: they can start from nothing, from inexperience, from the status of an insignificant player in the emerging Fourth Power.

Family, the Most Sustainable Resource of the Fourth Power

In bringing this modest book to a close, I wish to suggest that there are enormous resources not fully tapped and ready for use by China and the Fourth Power. It would be a strategic blunder for any nation, any economic organization, and any political leader to underestimate the resources that China and the Fourth Power have at their disposal—the sheer size of this potential market, the talents of 1.2 billion people, the unmatched richness of their cultural legacy. My guess is that all eyes will be on these resources, but one may be missed, the most important one, that is, the Chinese family—the most sustainable resource of China and the Fourth Power. Remember: the Great Wall may be in ruins, but not the Chinese family, at least not yet. As long as there is a Chinese family, there is hope for China and the Fourth Power.

APPENDICES

Appendix I

Administrative Divisions of the People's Republic of China

In land area, China ranks the third in the world - next only to Russia and Canada, and is slightly larger than the United States. Its 9.6 million square kilometer territory extends about 5,200 kilometers from west to east. From north to south, it measures some 5,500 kilometers. China has 31 divisions on the provincial level: 3 municipalities, 5 autonomous regions (where mostly ethnic minorities live) and 23 provinces.

Municipalities (3)	Abbreviations	Capitals of Autonomous Regions and Provinces
Beijing	Jing	
Shanghai	Hu	
Tianjin	Jin	
Autonomous Regions (5)		
Guangxi Zhuangzu Zizhiqu	Gui	Nanning
Nei Monggol Zizhiqu	Nei Mong	Huhhot
Ningxia Huizu Zizhiqu	Ning	Yinchuan
Xinjiang Uygur Zizhiqu	Xin	Urumqi
Xizang (Tibet) Zizhiqu	Zang	Lhasa
Provinces (23)		
Anhui	Wan	Hefei
Fujian	Min	Fuzhou
Gansu	Gan or Long	Lanzhou
Guangdong	Yue	Guangzhou
Guizhou	Gui or Qian	Guiyang
Hainan	N/A	Haikou
Hebei	Ji	Shijiazhuang
Henan	Yu	Zhengzhou
Heilongjiang	Hei	Harbin
Hubei	E	Wuhan
Hunan	Xiang	Changsha
Jiangsu	Su	Nanjing
Jiangxi	Gan	Nanchang
Jilin	Ji	Changchun
Liaoning	Liao	Shenyang
Qinghai	Qing	Xining
Shandong	Lu	Jinan
Shaanxi	Shaan	Xian
Shanxi	Jin	Taiyuan
Sichuan	Chuan or Shu	Chengdu
Taiwan	Tai	Taibei
Yunnan	Yun or Dian	Kunming
Zhejiang	Zhe	Hangzhou

Hierarchical Structure of the Chinese Government

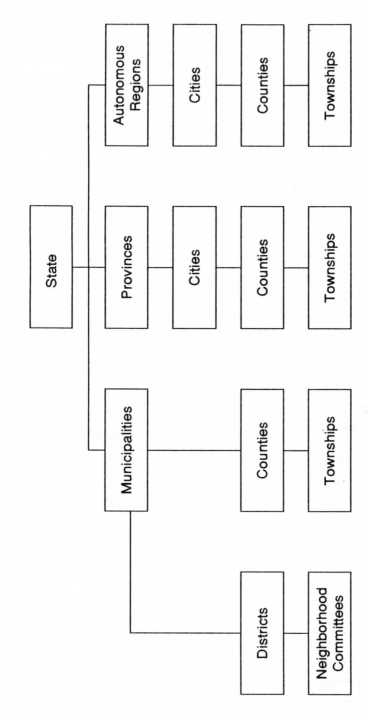

Appendix II

Main Social and Economic Indicators of the People's Republic of China

1. Natural Conditions

Items	Unit	1993
Land Area		
Surface Area of Country	(10,000 sq. km)	960
Surface Area of Sea	(10,000 sq. km)	473
Average Depth of Sea	(m)	961
Maximum Depth of Sea	(m)	5,377
Length of Coastline	(km)	32,000
Mainland Shore	(km)	18,000
Island Shore	(km)	14,000
Number of Islands		5,400
Area of Islands	(10,000 sq. km)	3.87
Climate		
Distribution of Thermal Energy		
Northern Heilongjiang and Tibet Plateau	(°C)	2,000-2,500
Northeast Plain	(°C)	3,000-4,000
Northern China Plain	(°C)	4,000-5,000
Changjiang River Drainage Area	(°C)	5,800-6,000
and Related Southern Area		
South Nanling Mountain Area	(°C)	7,000-8,000
Precipitation	(mm)	
Mid-Taiwan Mountain Area		>=4,000
Southern China Coastal Area		1,600-2,000
Changjiang River Drainage Area		1,000-1,500
Northern and Northeastern Area		400-800
Northwestern Inland		100-200
Talimu Basin, Tulufan Basin and Chaidamu Basin		<=25
Percentage of Climate Zones to Total Surface Area		
Tropical Climate Zone (aridity <1.0)		32
Semi-Tropical Climate Zone (aridity 1.0-1.5)		15
Semi-Arid Climate Zone (aridity 1.5-2.0)		22
Arid Climate Zone (aridity>2.0)		31

Note:

* Figures obtained from statistical checks during previous years, and are therefore subject to further verification and surveys.

2. Natural Resources

Item	Unit	1993
Land Resources	**(10,000 hectares)**	
Cultivated Land		9,510
Undeveloped Land		10,800
Useable		3,535
Afforestated Land		26,289
Developed Afforestated Land		6,303
Prairie		40,000
Utilizable		31,333
Forest		
Growing Stock	(100,000,000 cu. m)	108.68
Forest Area	(10,000 hectares)	12,863
Forest Growing Stock	(100,000,000 cu. m)	93..1
Forest-Cover Rate	(%)	13.4
Hydrology and Water Conservancy		
Land		
Earth Surface Water Volume	(100,000,000 cu. m)	28,124
Surface River Flow		27,115
Melted Glaciers		560
Underground Water Volume		8,287
Hydropower Resources	(100,000,000 kw)	6.76
Developable Resources		3.79
Inland Water Area	(10,000 hectares)	1,747
Cultivatable Area		675
Cultivated Area		416
Sea		
Theoretical Sea-energy Resources	(100,000,000 kw)	6.3
Coastal Area	(10,000 sq. km)	28
Sea/Beach Area	(10,000 sq. km)	2.08
Cultivatable Area in Marine Areas	(10,000 hectares)	260.01
Cultivated Area	(10,000 hectares)	58.8
Sea/beach Cultivable Area	(10,000 hectares)	242.0
Cultivated Area	(10,000 hectares)	43.3
Mineral Resources	**(100,000,000 ton)**	
Coal Reserves		10,018.65
Iron Ore Reserves		487.29
Phosphate Ore		157.66
Sylvite		4.58
Salt		4,024.00

Note:
* Figures for natural resources exclude Taiwan.
* Figures for land and hydrology water conservancy in this table were obtained from statistical checks during previous years. The figures are subject to further verification.
* Figures for forest resources were taken from the Third Census (1988–1992).

3. Gross National Products and Indices

Year	Gross National Products	Gross Domestic Products	Primary Industry	Secondary Industry	Industry	Construction	Tertiary Industry	Transporta-tion Post and Telecommuni-cations Services	Commerce	Per Capita GNP (Yuan)
Value (100,000, 000 Yuan)										
1978	3,588.1	3,588.1	1,018.4	1,745.2	1,607.0	138.2	824.5	172.8	265.5	375
1980	4,470.0	4,470.0	1,359.4	2,192.0	1,996.5	195.5	918.6	205.0	213.6	456
1983	5,809.0	5,787.0	1,960.8	2,646.2	2,375.6	270.6	1,180.0	264.9	171.0	568
1984	6,962.0	6,928.2	2,295.5	3,105.7	2,789.0	316.7	1,527.0	327.1	285.1	671
1985	8,557.6	8,527.4	2,541.6	3,866.6	3,448.7	417.9	2,119.2	406.9	577.0	814
1986	9,696.3	9,687.6	2,763.9	4,492.7	3,967.0	525.7	2,431.0	475.6	596.6	909
1987	11,301.0	11,307.1	3,204.3	5,251.6	4,585.8	665.8	2,851.2	544.9	714.2	1,042
1988	14,068.2	14,074.2	3,831.0	6,587.2	5,777.2	810.0	3,656.0	661.0	980.0	1,277
1989	15,993.3	15,997.6	4,228.0	7,278.0	6,484.0	794.0	4,491.6	786.0	1,012.0	1,430
1990	17,695.3	17,681.3	5,017.0	7,717.4	6,858.0	859.4	4,946.9	1,117.6	837.0	1,559
1991	20,236.3	20,188.3	5,288.6	9,102.2	8,087.1	1,015.1	5,797.5	1,277.0	1,245.5	1,758
1992	24,378.9	24,362.9	5,800.0	11,699.5	10,284.5	1,415.0	6,863.4	1,535.9	1,449.3	2,093
1993	31,342.3	31,380.3	6,650.0	16,244.9	14,140.0	2,104.9	8,485.4	1,901.0	1,782.4	2,663
Indices (1978 =100)										
1978	100.0	100.0	100.0	100.0	100.0	100.0	100.0	100.0	100.0	100.0
1980	116.0	116.0	104.6	122.9	122.4	129.2	114.3	113.8	107.4	113.1
1983	145.5	144.9	135.1	145.8	144.5	161.4	152.3	142.5	134.8	135.9
1984	166.9	166.0	152.6	166.9	166.7	179.0	178.3	163.8	153.6	153.9
1985	188.2	187.4	155.4	197.9	196.2	218.7	207.9	185.9	188.5	171.2
1986	203.5	203.3	160.5	218.2	215.2	253.4	231.0	209.7	201.1	182.4
1987	225.7	225.9	168.1	248.1	243.6	297.8	260.8	230.7	222.5	199.1
1988	251.2	251.3	172.3	284.1	280.8	322.5	296.2	261.5	250.3	218.0
1989	262.1	262.2	177.6	294.8	295.0	295.3	316.2	273.8	227.4	224.1
1990	272.7	272.4	190.7	304.1	304.9	298.8	323.0	297.2	2131	229.7
1991	295.0	294.2	195.2	344.7	346.9	327.4	340.8	322.5	220.5	244.6
1992	334.5	334.2	204.4	419.8	422.9	396.2	371.1	356.7	226.2	274.4
1993	378.7	379.0	212.6	505.4	512.1	455.6	405.6	393.8	242.9	307.1
Indices (Preced-ing year= 100)										
1978	111.7	111.7	104.1	115.0	116.4	99.4	113.8	108.9	123.1	110.2
1980	107.9	107.9	98.5	113.6	112.7	126.7	106.0	105.7	98.7	106.5
1983	110.4	110.2	108.3	110.4	109.7	117.1	112.6	110.0	112.4	108.8
1984	114.7	114.5	112.9	114.5	114.9	110.9	117.1	115.0	113.9	113.2
1985	112.8	112.9	101.8	118.6	118.2	122.2	116.6	113.5	122.7	111.3
1986	108.1	108.5	103.3	110.2	109.6	115.9	111.1	112.8	106.7	106.6
1987	110.9	111.1	104.7	113.7	113.2	117.9	112.9	110.0	110.6	109.1
1988	111.3	111.3	102.5	114.5	115.3	108.0	113.6	113.3	112.5	109.5
1989	104.4	104.3	103.1	103.8	105.1	91.6	106.7	104.7	90.9	102.8
1990	104.1	103.9	107.3	103.2	103.4	101.2	102.1	108.6	93.7	102.5
1991	108.2	108.0	102.4	113.3	113.8	109.6	105.5	108.5	103.5	106.7
1992	113.4	113.6	104.7	121.8	121.9	121.0	108.9	110.6	102.6	112.2
1993	113.2	113.4	104.0	120.4	121.1	115.0	109.3	110.4	107.4	111.8

Note:
* The balance between total of primary, secondary, tertiary industry and gross national products are net factor income from abroad.

4. Population and Its Composition (Year-End)

Year	Total Population	Male		Female		Urban		Rural	
		Population	(%)	Population	(%)	Population	(%)	Population	(%)
1952	57,482	29,833	51.90	27,649	48.10	7,163	12.46	50,319	87.54
1957	64,653	33,469	51.77	31,184	48.23	9,949	15.39	54,704	84.61
1962	67,295	34,517	51.29	32,778	48.71	11,659	17.33	55,636	82.67
1965	72,538	37,128	51.18	35,410	48.82	13,045	17.98	59,493	82.02
1970	82,992	42,686	51.43	40,306	48.57	14,424	17.38	68,568	82.62
1975	92,420	47,564	51.47	44,856	48.53	16,030	17.34	76,390	82.66
1978	96,259	49,567	51.49	46,692	48.51	17,245	17.92	79,014	82.08
1980	98,705	50,785	51.45	47,920	48.55	19,140	19.39	79,565	80.61
1983	103,008	53,152	51.60	49,856	48.40	22,274	21.62	80,734	78.38
1984	104,357	53,848	51.60	50,509	48.40	24,017	23.01	80,340	76.99
1985	105,851	54,725	51.70	51,126	48.30	25,094	23.71	80,757	76.29
1986	107,507	55,581	51.70	51,926	48.30	26,366	24.52	81,141	75.48
1987	109,300	56,290	51.50	53,010	48.50	27,674	25.32	81,626	74.68
1988	111,026	57,201	51.52	53,825	48.48	28,661	25.81	82,365	74.19
1989	112,704	58,099	51.55	54,605	48.45	29,540	26.21	83,164	73.79
1990	114,333	58,904	51.52	55,429	48.48	30,191	26.41	84,142	73.59
1991	115,823	59,466	51.34	56,357	48.66	30,543	26.37	85,280	73.63
1992	117,171	59811	51.05	57,360	48.95	32,372	27.63	84,799	72.37
1993	118,517	60,472	51.02	58,045	48.98	33,351	28.14	85,166	71.86

Note:

* Figures since 1982 were estimated based on the Fourth National Population Census (1990).

5. Basic Statistics on the Fourth National Population Census

Item	1953	1964	1982	1990
Total Population	**58,260**	**69,122**	**100,391**	**113,051**
Male	30,179	35,479	51,528	58,182
Female	28,081	33,643	48,863	54,869
Women at Childbearing age	13,314	15,161	24,849	30,635
Total Households	**13,411**	**15,671**	**22,115**	**27,862**
Family			22,008	27,691
Non-Family			107	171
Population by Age				
Age 0-6	11,700	13,542	13,456	15,548
Age 7-14	8,884	14,525	20,269	15,752
Population within Working Age	29,983	34,149	55,087	67,903
Males Age 60 and Females Age 55 and over	5,170	5,407	9,304	11,684
Nationality Population	**58,260**	**69,122**	**100,391**	**113,051**
Han Nationality	54,728	65,130	93,667	103,919
Minority Nationality	3,532	3,992	6,724	9,132
Marital Status of Population Age 15 and Over			**66,548**	**81,751**
Unmarried			19,012	20,541
Married			42,376	55,737
Widowed			4,764	4,989
Divorced			396	484
Population Age 6 and Over By Educational Level		**55,542**	**88,979**	**99,409**
University		287	604	614
Junior College				962
Technical Secondary School				1,728
Senior Middle School		912	6,653	7,260
Junior Middle School		3,235	17,820	26,339
Primary School		19,582	35,534	42,021
Illiterate and Semi-Illiterate		31,526	28,368	20,485
Employed Population			**52,150**	**64,724**
Unemployed Population			**14,516**	**17,026**
Population of Cities, Towns and Counties	**58,260**	**69,122**	**100,391**	**113,051**
City			14,525	21,122
Town	7,726	9,455	6,106	8,492
County	50,534	59,667	79,760	83,437

Note:

* Figures in this table refers to population on mainland, excluding Hong Kong, Taiwan and military personnel.

* Working age range refers to 16–59 for men and 16–54 for women.

* Excluding population age 15 and population whose true age is unknown, so population by age all together is not equal to total population.

* Figures for 1964 refer to population age 7 and over. Including children not in school. Excluding 4.75 million persons whose education level are unknown.

6. Employment by Type of Industry

(Year-End)	Number of Employees (10,000)				Percentage (Total=100)		
Year Region	Total	Primary Industry	Secondary Industry	Tertiary Industry	Primary Industry	Secondary Industry	Tertiary Industry
1952	20,729	17,316	1,528	1,885	83.5	7.4	9.1
1957	23771	19,300	2,115	2,356	81.2	8.9	9.9
1962	25,910	21,259	2,033	2,618	82.0	7.8	10.1
1965	28,670	23,372	2,376	2,922	81.5	8.3	10.2
1970	34,432	27,786	3,479	3,167	80.7	10.1	9.2
1975	38,168	29,415	5,075	3,678	77.1	13.3	9.6
1978	40,152	28,313	6,970	4,869	70.5	17.4	12.1
1980	42,361	29,117	7,736	5,508	68.7	18.3	13.0
1983	46,436	31,145	8,711	6,580	67.1	18.8	14.2
1984	48,197	30,862	9,622	7,713	64.0	20.0	16.0
1985	49,873	31,105	10,418	8,350	62.4	20.9	16.7
1986	51,282	31,212	11,251	8,819	60.9	21.9	17.2
1987	52,783	31,614	11,762	9,407	59.9	22.3	17.8
1988	54,334	32,197	12,188	9,949	59.3	22.4	18.3
1989	55,329	33,170	12,012	10,147	60.0	21.7	18.3
1990	56,740	34,049	12,158	10,533	60.0	21.4	18.6
1991	58,360	34,876	12,469	11,015	59.8	21.4	18.9
1992	59,432	34,769	12,921	11,742	58.5	21.7	19.8
1993	60,220	33,966	13,517	12,737	56.4	22.4	21.2
Beijing	659	78	278	286	11.8	42.2	43.4
Tianjin	478	89	235	144	18.6	49.1	30.2
Hebei	3,241	1,857	772	587	57.3	23.8	18.1
Shanxi	1,414	642	419	331	45.4	29.7	23.4
Inner Mongolia	999	534	213	219	53.5	21.3	22.0
Liaoning	1,952	631	780	470	32.3	40.0	24.1
Jilin	1,230	578	344	263	46.9	27.9	21.4
Heilongjiang	1,492	569	523	337	38.1	35.0	22.6
Shanghai	740	68	407	252	9.2	55.0	34.0
Jiangsu	3,743	1,657	1,247	802	44.3	33.3	21.4
Zhejiang	2,659	1,248	782	578	46.9	29.4	21.7
Anhui	3,049	1,961	501	535	64.3	16.4	17.6
Fujian	1,521	820	341	315	53.9	22.4	20.7
Jiangxi	1,893	1,089	341	420	57.5	18.0	22.2
Shandong	4,473	2,610	1,044	772	58.4	23.3	17.3
Henan	4,481	2,915	790	725	65.0	17.6	16.2
Hubei	2,607	1,479	542	544	56.7	20.8	20.9
Hunan	3,361	2,206	512	583	65.6	15.2	17.3
Guangdong	3,480	1,497	923	917	43.0	26.5	26.3
Guangxi	2,277	1,594	249	394	70.0	10.9	17.3
Hainan	320	208	33	59	65.1	10.4	18.5
Sichuan	6,221	4,148	957	1,054	66.7	15.4	16.9
Guizhou	1,770	1,374	162	208	77.6	9.2	11.8
Yunnan	2,106	1,630	201	255	77.4	9.6	12.1
Tibet	113	88	5	17	77.3	4.0	14.8
Shaanxi	1,718	1,061	328	305	61.8	19.1	17.7
Gansu	1,131	692	194	231	61.1	17.1	20.4
Qinghai	217	131	41	41	60.2	18.6	18.8
Ningxia	230	140	43	43	61.0	18.8	18.5
Xinjiang	646	375	119	127	58.0	18.4	19.6

7. Possession of Major Durable Consumer Goods

Items	Unit	1985	1990	1991	1992
Possession of Durable Consumer Goods					
Sewing Machines	(10,000)	9,833	14,055	14,544	14,966
Bicycles	(10,000)	22,364	39,099	41,979	45,076
Electric Fans	(10,000)	6,360	20,127	22,989	25,774
Washing Machines	(10,000)	3,030	9,628	10,615	11,709
Refrigerators	(10,000)	410	2,996	3,466	3,941
Television Sets	(10,000)	6,965	18,546	20,671	22,843
Tape Recorders	(10,000)	3,660	11,875	13,099	14,305
Radios	(10,000)	24,181	25,123	23,399	21,595
Cameras	(10,000)	1,186	2,275	2,465	2,663
Possession of Durable Consumer Goods per 100 Persons					
Sewing Machines		9.3	12.3	12.6	12.8
Bicycles		21.1	34.2	36.2	38.5
Electric Fans		6.0	17.6	19.8	22.0
Washing Machines		2.9	8.4	9.2	10.0
Refrigerators		0.4	2.6	3.0	3.4
Television Sets		6.6	16.2	17.8	19.5
Tape Recorders		3.5	10.4	11.3	12.2
Radios		22.8	22.0	20.2	18.4
Cameras		1.1	2.0	2.1	2.3

8. Basic Indicators of Urban Households from Sample Survey

Item	Unit	1985	1990	1991	1992	1993
Households Surveyed	(Households)	24,338	35,660	36,730	36,290	35,390
Average Persons per Household	(Persons)	3.89	3.50	3.43	3.37	3.31
Average Employees Per Household	(Persons)	2.15	1.98	1.96	1.95	1.92
Percentage of Employment per Household	(%)	55.27	56.57	57.14	57.86	58.00
Persons Supported by Each Employee (including the employee himself)	(Persons)	1.81	1.77	1.75	1.73	1.72
Annual Income Per Capita	(Yuan)	748.92	1,522.79	1,713.10	2,031.53	2,583.16
Per Capita Income Available for Living		685.32	1,387.27	1,544.30	1,826.07	2,336.54
Wages of Staff and Workers in State-Owned Units		455.88	857.59	969.69	1,242.94	1,548.53
Wages of Staff and Workers in Collective-Owned Units		113.52	170.39	177.89	209.50	230.24
Other Income of Staff and Workers		44.88	99.11	116.90	133.00	178.51
Income of Individual Laborers		10.20	18.71	25.06	28.58	40.67
Reemployment Income of Retirees		4.56	15.51	15.94	20.81	26.82
Income of Other Employees		1.95	3.79	5.4	3.60	4.81
Part-Time Income		12.36	22.61	27.22	32.97	53.57
Interest, Dividends and Rent		3.74	15.60	19.72	30.53	45.80
Pensions, Subsidies, Donations and Other		65.88	250.01	274.40	237.44	325.75
Special Income		35.95	69.46	80.86	92.16	108.08
Annual Living Expenditures Per Capita	(Yuan)	673.20	1,278.89	1,453.81	1,671.73	2,110.81
Food		351.72	693.77	782.50	884.82	1,058.20
Clothing		98.04	170.90	199.64	240.60	300.61
Daily-Use Articles		71.88	129.66	139.83	161.98	246.54
Cultural and Recreational Activities		51.96	68.25	68.68	74.04	70.18
Books, Newspapers and Magazines		6.12	11.15	13.11	16.14	18.92
House Rent		6.48	9.43	10.66	14.33	22.00
Water and Electricity		6.84	19.81	24.16	28.58	38.26
Gas			2.62	4.27	5.42	8.99

9. Basic Indicators of Rural Households

Item	1980	1985	1990	1991	1992	1993
Households Surveyed	15,914	66,642	66,960	67,410	67,490	67,570
Residents Surveyed (Persons)						
Permanent Residents in the Household Surveyed	88,090	341,525	321,429	317,816	315,036	310,194
Average Permanent Residents Per Household	5.54	5.12	4.80	4.71	4.67	4.59
Average Full-Time and Part-Time Laborers Per Household	2.45	2.95	2.92	2.83	2.83	2.87
Average Persons Supported by Each Laborers (including the laborer himself or herself)	2.26	1.74	1.64	1.66	1.65	1.60
Average Per Capita Annual Income (Yuan)						
Total Revenue	216.22	547.31	990.38	1,046.10	1,155.38	1,333.82
Net Income	191.33	397.60	686.31	708.55	783.99	921.62
Cash Income	113.12	357.39	676.67	736.84	808.16	910.15
Percentage of Households by Per Capita Annual Net Income (%)						
Below 100 Yuan	9.80	0.96	0.22	0.40	0.34	0.45
100-150	24.70	3.40	0.51	0.77	0.53	0.38
150-200	27.10	7.86	1.29	1.56	1.12	0.78
200-300	25.30	25.61	6.57	6.64	5.63	3.41
300-400	8.60	24.00	11.99	11.08	9.93	6.33
400-500	2.90	15.85	14.37	13.35	12.65	9.05
500-600	9.06	13.99	13.00	12.56	12.98	10.38
600-800	8.02	20.83	20.90	21.21	21.44	20.28
800-1,000	2.93	12.45	12.83	14.19	13.83	15.77
1,000-1,500	1.89	12.20	12.99	15.32	14.15	19.35
1,500-2,000	0.26	3.47	3.89	4.82	4.10	7.06
2,000 Yuan and Over	0.16	2.11	2.59	4.06	3.29	6.76
Average Per Capita Annual Expenditures (Yuan)						
Total Expenditures	195.52	485.51	903.47	979.64	1,055.91	1,211.18
Household Business Expenditures	24.61	121.39	241.09	267.27	292.28	330.03
Living Expenditures	162.21	317.42	584.63	619.79	659.01	769.65
Other Nonproductive Expenditures	8.42	9.57	18.80	23.28	27.45	24.45
Cash Expenditures	122.93	389.19	741.17	830.19	895.44	1,005.77
Productive Costs	14.05	98.93	183.35	215.09	236.21	275.67
Taxes and Payments to Collectives	0.24	16.35	33.38	36.19	41.08	42.06
Consumption Expenditures	83.83	194.68	374.74	404.74	431.37	490.14
Savings and Credit Expenditures	15.91	57.96	102.11	116.79	126.23	136.29

10. Number of National Cities (1993)
(Grouped by Population)

Region	Total	2,000,000 and over	1,000,000-2,000-000	500,000-1,000,000	200,000-500,000	Below 200,000
National	570	10	22	36	160	342
Beijing	1	1				
Tianjin	1	1				
Hebei	30		2	3	4	21
Shanxi	17		1	1	3	12
Inner Mongolia	17		1	1	4	11
Liaoning	28	1	3	5	7	12
Jilin	25		2		10	13
Heilongjiang	29	1	1	6	9	12
Shanghai	1	1		4		
Jiangsu	35	1		1	13	17
Zhejiang	31		1	2	3	26
Anhui	19			1	10	7
Fujian	20				4	15
Jiangxi	18		1		5	12
Shandong	43		3	2	17	21
Henan	31		1	3	8	19
Hubei	31	1		1	9	20
Hunan	28		1	1	6	20
Guangdong	38	1		2	19	16
Guangxi	14			2	3	9
Hainan	5				1	4
Sichuan	31	1	1		12	17
Guizhou	11		1		2	8
Yunnan	14		1		2	11
Tibet	2					2
Shaanxi	13	1			3	9
Gansu	13		1		2	10
Qinghai	3			1		2
Ningxia	4				2	2
Xinjiang	17		1		2	14

11. Utilization of Foreign Capital

(US $ 100,000,000)	Total		Foreign Loans		Direct Foreign Investments		Others
Year	Number of Contracts	Value	Number of Contracts	Value	Number of Contracts	Value	Other Foreign Investment
Total Value of Foreign Capital Through Signed Contracts Agreements							
1979-1982	949	205.48	27	135.49	922	60.10	9.89
1983	522	34.30	52	15.13	470	17.32	1.85
1984	1,894	47.91	38	19.16	1,856	26.51	2.24
1985	3,145	98.67	72	35.34	3,073	59.32	4.01
1986	1,551	117.37	53	84.07	1,498	28.34	4.96
1987	2,289	121.36	56	78.17	2,233	37.09	6.10
1988	6,063	160.04	118	98.13	5,945	52.97	8.94
1989	5,909	114.79	130	51.85	5,779	56.00	6.94
1990	7,371	120.86	98	50.99	7,273	65.96	3.91
1991	13,086	195.83	108	71.61	12,978	119.77	4.45
1992	48,858	694.39	94	107.03	48,764	581.24	6.12
1993	83,595	1,232.73	158	113.06	83,437	1,114.36	5.31
Total Value of Foreign Capital Used							
1979-1982		124.57		106.90		11.66	6.01
1983		19.81		10.65		6.36	2.80
1984		27.05		12.86		12.58	1.61
1985		46.47		26.88		16.61	2.98
1986		72.58		50.14		18.74	3.70
1987		84.52		58.05		23.14	3.33
1988		102.26		64.87		31.94	5.45
1989		100.59		62.86		33.92	3.81
1990		102.89		65.34		34.87	2.68
1991		115.54		68.88		43.66	3.00
1992		192.02		79.11		110.07	2.84
1993		389.60		111.89		275.15	2.56

Note:
* For using different units and decimal place in data collection, sum of figures for some years do not equal to total.

12. Utilization of Foreign Capital Through Signed Contracts or Agreements by Investment

(US $ 10,000)	1992		1993	
Item	Number of Contracts	Value	Number of Contracts	Value
Total	48,858	6,943,873	83,595	12,327,273
Foreign Loans	94	1,070,328	158	1,130,571
Government Loans	75	438,972	132	288,971
Loans from International Monetary Organizations	19	217,171	26	380,779
Other		414,185		460,821
Direct Foreign Investments	48,764	5,812,351	83,437	11,143,566
Joint Venture	34,354	2,912,846	54,003	5,517,427
Cooperative Operation	5,711	1,325,548	10,445	2,549,998
Cooperative Development	7	4,340	14	30,462
Foreign Enterprise	8,692	1,569,617	18,975	3,045,679
Other Foreign Investments		61,194		53,136
Compensation Trade		41,466		6,562
Processing and Assembly		11,987		27,002
International Rents		7,741		19,572

Note:

* Other foreign investments include value of equipment supplied by foreign businesses in transactions involving compensation trade, processing and assembly, and the value of equipment supplied in financial leasing transactions.

13. Basic Statistics for Education

Item	1980	1985	1990	1992	1993
Number of Schools					
Institutions of Higher Education	675	1,016	1,075	1,053	1,065
Secondary Schools	124,760	104,848	100,777	97,784	96,744
Specialized Secondary Schools	3,069	3,557	3,982	3,903	3,964
Regular Secondary Schools	118,377	93,221	87,631	84,021	82,795
Primary Schools	917,316	832,309	766,072	712,973	696,681
Number of Full-Time Teachers (10,000 Persons)					
Institutions of Higher Education	24.7	34.4	39.5	38.8	38.8
Secondary Schools	317.1	296.7	349.2	362.4	366.8
Specialized Secondary Schools	12.8	17.4	23.4	23.5	23.9
Regular Secondary Schools	302.0	265.2	303.3	314.1	316.7
Primary Schools	549.9	537.7	558.2	552.7	555.2
New Student Enrollment (10,000 Persons)					
Institutions of Higher Education	28.1	61.9	60.9	75.4	92.4
Secondary Schools	2,011.8	1,789.8	1,815.8	1,939.8	1,983.7
Specialized Secondary Schools	46.8	66.8	73.0	87.9	114.9
Regular Secondary Schools	1,934.3	1,606.9	1,619.6	1,699.7	1,707.3
Primary Schools	2,942.3	2,298.2	2,064.0	2,183.2	2,353.5
Student Enrollment (10,000 Persons)					
Institutions of Higher Education	114.4	170.3	206.3	218.4	253.6
Secondary Schools	5,677.8	5,092.6	5,105.4	5,354.4	5,383.7
Specialized Secondary Schools	124.3	157.1	224.4	240.8	282.0
Regular Secondary Schools	5,508.1	4,706.0	4,586.0	4,770.8	4,739.1
Primary Schools	14,627.0	13,370.2	12,241.4	12,201.3	12,421.2
Graduates (10,000 Persons)					
Institutions of Higher Education	14.7	31.6	61.4	60.4	57.1
Secondary Schools	1,629.9	1,279.1	1,479.5	1,499.4	1,541.9
Specialized Secondary Schools	41.0	42.9	66.1	74.3	73.6
Regular Secondary Schools	1,581.0	1,194.9	1,342.1	1,328.4	1,365.9
Primary Schools	2,053.3	1,999.9	1,863.1	1,872.4	1,841.5
Student - Teacher Ratio					
Institutions of Higher Education	4.6	5.0	5.2	5.6	6.5
Secondary Schools	17.9	17.2	14.6	14.8	14.7
Primary	26.6	24.9	21.9	22.1	22.4
Government Expenditures on Education (100,000,000 Yuan)					
Budgetary Education Expenditures			548.7	728.8	
Administration Expenditures			426.1	538.7	
Capital Construction investment in Education			352.5	454.0	
			29.6	33.8	

14. Basic Statistics on Marriage Registrations and Divorces

Year	Total Registered Marriages (Couples)	First Marriages (Persons)	Remarriages (Persons)	Divorces (Couples)	Divorce Rate
1980	7,197,860	13,903,379	492,341	340,998	0.7
1985	8,312,837	16,118,979	506,695	457,938	0.9
1986	8,839,786	17,106,622	572,950	505,675	0.9
1987	9,267,456	17,918,352	616,560	581,484	1.1
1988	8,991,771	17,321,736	661,806	658,551	1.2
1989	9,372,304	17,928,312	816,296	752,914	1.3
1990	9,510,632	18,233,452	787,812	800,037	1.4
1991	9,509,849	18,203,226	816,472	829,449	1.4
1992	9,545,047	18,320,957	769,137	849,611	1.5
1993	9,121,622	17,470,092	773,152	909,195	1.5

Appendix III

Main Social and Economic Indicators of Taiwan

1. Main Indicators of Area and Population

		1980	1990	1991	1992
Area	(10,000 sq.km)	3.6	3.6	3.6	3.6
Year-End Population	(10,000)	1,780.5	2,035.3	2,055.7	2,075.2
Male		922.8	1,051.6	1,061.5	1,070.8
Female		851.7	983.7	994.2	1,004.4
Crude Birth Rate	(‰)	23.4	16.6	15.7	15.5
Crude Death Rate	(‰)	4.8	5.2	5.2	5.3
Infant Mortality Rate	(‰)	11.0	5.9	5.4	5.6
Fertility Rate	(‰)	91.0	62.0	58.0	57.0
Natural Growth Rate	(‰)	18.6	11.4	10.5	10.2
Marriage Rate	(‰)	9.9	7.1	8.0	8.2
Divorce Rate	(‰)	0.8	1.4	1.4	1.4
Life Expectancy at Birth	(Year)		73.8	74.3	74.3
Male		69.6	71.3	71.8	71.8
Female		75.5	76.8	77.2	77.2
Age-Specific Distribution	(%)				25.8
0-14 Year		32.1	27.1	26.3	67.4
14-64 Year		63.6	66.7	67.2	6.8
65 Year and Over		4.3	6.2	6.5	
Non-Agricultural Population As		69.7			80.3
% of Total Population	(%)		78.8	79.5	
Population Density (Persons/sq.km)		494.6	565.4	571.0	576.5

2. Gross National Products

Year	Gross National Products			Per Capita Gross National Products	
	(NT $ 1000,000,000)	Annual Growth Rate of Change (%)	(US $ 100,000,000)	NT $	US $
1989	39,690	7.3	1,503	198,389	7,512
1990	43,270	5.0	1,609	213,888	7,954
1991	48,212	7.2	1,798	235,699	8,788
1992	53,017	6.0	2,107	256,682	10,202
1993	58,093	5.9	2.201	278,821	10,566

3. Percentage of Families Owning Household Appliances

Year	Color TV	Refrigerator	Air Conditioner	Washing Machine	Telephone	Automobile	Family Computer
1982	83.12	94.33	17.16	70.52	67.65	7.23	
1983	87.79	95.44	19.72	73.68	74.35	9.30	1.46
1984	90.41	96.13	22.91	75.49	80.51	10.38	1.94
1985	92.31	96.67	23.95	77.84	82.12	11.91	2.32
1986	94.42	97.11	25.45	79.49	85.25	13.63	2.92
1987	95.78	97.41	28.66	81.33	87.20	15.54	3.55
1988	97.34	97.93	34.29	83.97	89.11	19.21	3.95
1989	97.80	98.25	41.74	86.82	91.51	24.90	5.42
1990	98.26	98.37	47.26	88.79	93.08	29.07	6.77
1991	99.16	98.96	52.37	89.53	94.75	33.67	9.57
1992	99.30	98.93	56.14	90.38	95.13	38.94	11.76

Appendix IV

Main Social and Economic Indicators of Hong Kong

1. Main Indicators of Population

		1980	1990	1991	1992
Area	(km.sq)				
Year-End Population	(10,000)	506.0	570.5	575.5	581.2
Birth Rate	(‰)	17.0	12.0	12.0	12.3
Death Rate	(‰)	5.0	5.2	5.0	5.3
Infant Mortality Rate	(‰)	11.2	6.2	6.4	4.8
Rate of Natural Increase	(‰)	12.0	6.8	7.0	7.0
Marriage Population	(Persons)	51,111	47,168	42,568	45,702
Divorce Decree	(Persons)	2,421	5,551	6,295	5,650
Life Expectancy at Birth	(Years)				
Male		71.6	74.6	75.1	75.1
Female		77.9	80.3	80.6	80.7

2. Gross Domestic Products

	Gross Domestic Products			Per Capita GDP	
Year	(HK $ 100,000,000)	Growth Rate (%)	(US $100,000,000)	HK $	US $
1988	4,337	8.3	526	77,059	9,250
1989	4,992	2.8	592	87,784	11,254
1990	5,596	3.2	667	97,968	12,578
1991	6,434	4.1	676	111,799	14,387
1992	7,474	5.3		128,613	16,615

Appendix V

China's Lunar-Calendar-Based Traditional Festivals and Solar-Calendar-Based Holidays

China's Lunar Calendar Based Traditional Festivals
and Solar Calendar Based Holidays

China's lunar calendar, which is said to have come into existence as early as the *Xia* Dynasty (about 2,100-1,700 B.C.), has been in use for several thousand years and is still in common use today.

There are many traditional festivals in China each year. Most of the festivals are related to certain stories which usually sing the praises of a historical figure, describe a mysterious legend or wish a harvest and happiness. All the traditional festivals are based on the Chinese lunar calendar which is about 20 to 30 days in difference with the solar calendar.

You will be lucky if you come to China on one of these festivals. You will get a glimpse of the long-standing culture, values and customs of the Chinese nation through the celebration of these traditional festivals. Based on the lunar calendar, China's main festivals are:

Spring Festival

This festival falls on the 1st day of the 1st lunar month, in late January or early February. It is by far the most important and celebrated holiday in China, usually celebrated with great pomp, feasting and merry making. In fact, it resembles everything of the Christmas in the West. It heralds the arrival of spring and the beginning of a new year. The whole family get together for an annual reunion dinner on the New Year's Eve. One of the dishes of the abundant and elaborate New Year's dinner as the last course is fish with which to wish a bumper harvest in the new year because fish is pronounced *Yu* which is similar to the pronunciation of *surplus* in Chinese. Tons of firecrackers are lit to drive away ghosts and bad luck of the past. Relatives and friends visit each other, wishing everybody good luck, a happy life, and a big fortune. Popular Spring Festival greetings are *Xinnian Hao!* (Happy New Year!), *Wanshi Ruyi!* (Good luck!) and *Gongxi Facai!* (Wish you a fortune!), and the like.

Lantern Festival

This festival is on the 5th day of the 1st lunar month, usually toward the end of February. The specialty for the occasion is sweet boiled dumplings made with glutinous rice flour. People hang out lanterns, do the lion dance, and shoot off firecrackers. This festival marks the traditional end of Spring Festival. After Lantern Festival, everything is back to normal and a new, busy working year begins.

Clear and Bright Day

This festival arrives at the end of the 2nd lunar month or one of the early days of the 3rd which tends to fall in early April. It is an occasion to remember the dead. Family members go to the tombs of the deceased to pay their respects and *saomu* (sweep the tomb). Since it comes in spring, people now often use the time for spring outings.

Dragon Boat Festival

This festival falls on the 5th day of the 5th lunar month, in late May or early June. People hold dragon boat competitions and make *zongzi* - a pyramid-shaped glutinous rice dumpling which is wrapped in bamboo or reed leaves. This tradition comes from the story of over 2,000 years ago about poet *Qu Yuan* of the ancient State of *Chu*. He was so deeply grieved when his country's capital city fell to the hands of invading enemy that he drowned himself in a river. To prevent his body from being eaten by fish and shrimp in the river out of respect for the poet, people made this special food to feed river creatures. Of course, now the dumplings are only a special snack eaten around this festival.

Mid-Autumn Festival

This festival is celebrated on the 15th day of the 8th lunar month, falling mostly in early September. At night of this day the moon is supposed to be brighter and fuller than that of any other months and the moonlight is the most beautiful. In China a full moon is also symbolic of family reunion, thus that day is also known as the day of reunion. Every family stays together to enjoy looking at the full moon while having a special kind of pastry called *yuebin* (moon-cake), a round cake stuffed with sweeten walnuts and dried fruits.

Solar Calendar Based Holidays

After the founding of the People's Republic of China in 1949, the Gregorian calendar, called the solar calendar in China, was adopted. The main holidays based on solar calendar are:

New Year's Day (January 1st)
International Working Women's Day (March 8th)
International Labor Day (May 1st)
Chinese Youth Day (May 4th)
International Children's Day (June 1st)
National Day (October 1st, Anniversary of the Founding of the People's Republic of China since 1949)

Appendix VI

Table of Chinese Dynasties

Wu Di Dynasty		C. 26 - 21 Century B.C.
Xia Dynasty		C. 21 - 17 Century B.C.
Shang Dynasty		C. 17 - 11 Century B. C
Zhou Dynasty (C. 11 Century B.C. - 256 B. C.)	Western *Zhou*	C. 11 Century B.C. - 771 B.C.
	Eastern *Zhou*	770 B.C. - 256 B.C.
	Spring & Autumn Period	770 B.C. - 476 B.C.
	Warring States Period	475 B.C. - 221 B.C.
Qin Dynasty		221 B.C. - 206 B.C.
Han Dynasties (206 B.C. - A.D. 220)	Western *Han*	206 B.C. - A.D. 25
	Eastern *Han*	25 - 220
Three Kingdoms (220 - 280)	*Wei*	220 - 265
	Shu Han	221 - 263
	Wu	222 - 280
Jin Dynasty (265 - 420)	Western *Jin*	265 - 317
	Eastern *Jin*	317 - 420
Southern - Northern Dynasties (420 - 589)	*Song*	420 - 479
	Qi	479 - 502
	Liang	502 - 557
	Chen	557 - 589
	Northern *Wei*	386 - 534
	Eastern *Wei*	534 - 550
	Northern *Qi*	550 - 577
	Western *Wei*	535 - 556
	Northern *Zhou*	557 - 581
Sui Dynasty		581 - 618
Tang Dynasty		618 - 907
Five Dynasties (907 - 960)	Late *Liang*	907 - 923
	Late *Tang*	923 - 936
	Late *Jin*	936 - 947
	Late *Han*	947 - 950
	Late *Zhou*	951 - 960
Song Dynasty (960 - 1279)	Northern *Song*	960 - 1127
	Southern *Song*	1127 - 1279
Liao Dynasty		970 - 1125
Jin Dynasty		1115 - 1234
Yuan Dynasty		1206 - 1368
Ming Dynasty		1368 - 1644
Qing Dynasty		1616 - 1911
Republic of China		1912 - 1949
The People's Republic of China		Founded since 1949 - present

NOTES

1. See *The Economist*, 28 November 1992.

2. Wei Jingsheng was actively involved in the Xidan Domocracy Wall Movement in Beijing in 1978. On charges of treason and engaging in counterrevolutionary activities, Wei was later arrested and sentenced to fifteen years imprisonment. The case became nationally and internationally known because of its political nature and the personal intervention by China's paramount leader Deng Xiaoping.

3. Wei was later put under house arrest due to his alleged involvement in pro-democracy activities.

4. The *New York Times* on 21 September 1993 published an editorial entitled "China Doesn't Deserve the Olympics," in which the editorial writer argued, using somewhat arrogant language, that China does not deserve to host the year 2000 Olympics becuase of its alleged human rights abuses.

5. "Blue ocean" is a term that was used in a controversial six-part television documentary *River Eulogy* aired in China in the summer of 1988. The term is used to refer to modern capitalism. Su Xiaokang, its co-author, because of his pro-democracy stance, fled to the United States after the Tienanmen crisis in June 1989.

6. Samuel P. Huntington in the Summer 1993 issue of *Foreign Affairs* published his controversial "The Clash of Civilizations?" in which he argues that "the fundamental source of conflict in this new world will not be primarily ideological or primarily economic. The great divisions among humankind and the dominating source of conflict will be cultural. Nation-states will remain the most powerful actors in world affairs, but the principal conflicts of global politics will occur between nations and groups of different civilizations. The clash of civilizations will dominate global politics. The faultlines between civilizations will be the battlelines of the future" (p. 22).

7. Japan in 1960 and Korea in 1984 were hosts of the Olympic Games, which brought enormous publicity, and respect, for

the two East Asian countries. Their economic success and increased influence in the world arena were believed to be instrumental in persuading the Olympic Committee to hold the games there.

8. In the Warring States period, King Gou Jian of Kingdom Yue was defeated by Kingdom Wu. Legend says that Gou Jian retreated to sleep on brushwood and taste gall to develop his will so that he could stage a comeback. Finally, Gou Jian succeeded in conquering Kingdom Wu. Later, "sleep on brushwood and taste gall," or *wo xin chang dan*, became an idiom, meaning where there is a will there is a way.

9. See *Business Week*, 28 November 1994, p. 66.

10. Those who are interested in a detailed discussion of how the Chinese family structure has remained solidly unshaken should read *The Great Wall in Ruins: Communication and Cultural Change in China*, which Godwin Chu and I co-authored. The book was published by SUNY Press in 1993.

11. *Xiahai* reads "go down to the ocean" in Chinese, a reference to going into business or, in an extended sense making extra money by working a second or third job. For a time, *xiahai* became a popular practice among professionals, diverting, for example, a professor's attention from teaching and research.

12. The article was carried in the 3 October 1993 *Time* magazine.

13. John Kao's article "The Worldwide Web of Chinese Business" appeared in the March-April 1993 issue of *Harvard Business Review*.

14. See the 18 July 1992 issue of *The Economist*.

15. Kenichi Ohmae's *The Borderless World: Power and Strategy in the Interlinked Economy* was published by McKinsey & Company in 1990.

16. It's been reported that the Chinese government does not encourage such terms as "the Fourth Power" or "Greater China" for fear that the West might believe that this may be a protectionist trade circle engineered by Beijing. I feel such fears are unfounded and quite unnecessary.

17. At the Third Plenary Session of the Eleventh Party Congress held in Beijing in December 1978, senior leader Deng

Xiaoping made a historical call for the Party to switch its work focus from class struggle to economic production, thus officially beginning the economic reform which is still going on. One may also say the reform actually began in 1979.

18. It seems that more and more people are realizing that further encouraging China to engage in international trade activities and stay as a full member of the international community is ten times more effective and meaningful than threatening the People's Republic with economic sanctions and other punitive measures. China is too large and proud for it to succumb to power politics. Economic and cultural co-operation is the best way to engage a 1.2 billion people nation.

19. This was calculated on a non-Purchasing-Power-Parities basis.

20. These studies were reported in the 18 July 1992 issue of *The Economist.*

21. I expect this trend to ease as non-Chinese sources increase their volume and speed of investing in China.

22. It is a shared perception among scholars from both Taiwan and the mainland that the latter represents a much larger pool of well-educated, high-calibre scientists. It is important for members of the Fourth Power to distribute this talent pool to achieve its own goals of going "upmarket."

23. See the April 1993 issue of *The Asian Business.*

24. See above.

25. The complete title of this is *To See Ourselves: Comparing Traditional Chinese and American Cultural Values.* The book was published by the Westview Press in 1994.

26. Please see the 30 October 1993 issue of *The Economist.*

27. I've observed and studied Chinese and American media behavior since 1978 when I started my advanced degree studies in international communication. It seems amazingly true that both the Chinese official press and the privately controlled American media tend to give biased, and often distorted, coverage of the other country's events.

28. Mr. Wu Bangguo and Mr. Huang Ju, both of whom have a close association with Party Secretary General Jiang Zemin, have become members of the powerful Politburo.

29. It's always amazing to me that the well-informed Western media, the American media in particular, simply cannot change the habit of calling the mainland *Communist* China or *Red* China. This can, indeed, be very misleading to the public simply because it's no longer true.

30. Bao-the-Judge, nicknamed *baoqintian* or clear-as-the-sky-Bao,was a legendary twelfth-century official who was a fair judge to all, regardless of their wealth or social position.

31. This is one of the biggest paradoxes in Chinese politics. The rule of benevolent authoritarianism cannot be guaranteed without successful systemic political reform while systemic reform cannot even happen without the approval of the benevolent authoritarian power structure.

32. See M. H. Chang, "China's Future: Regionalism, Federation, or Disintegration," *Studies in Comparative Communism* 25.3 (September 1992): 224.

33. This is a quote from *The Wisdom of Laotse*, p. 90. The book was edited by Lin Yutang and first copyrighted by Random House in 1948. The copyright was renewed in 1976 by the Modern Libr?

⌣⊣. See Tom Peters, *Thriving on Chaos* (New York: Harper & Row, 1989).

35. This is not the same as benevolent authoritarianism, which may or may not lead to the practice of man being above the law.

36. Lu Xun, one of the best-known essayists in contemporary China, has been known for his poignant satire and criticism of the suppressive nature of China's feudal system. In his *The Story of Ah Q*, one of his masterpieces, he created a prototypical Chinese peasant, called Ah Q, whose way of resisting the pressure from life and the larger feudal society is by creating illusions in which to make himself feel good psychologically. Lu Xun died in the 1930s.

37. See p. xi of Chu and Ju's *The Great Wall in Ruins: Communication and Cultural Change in China.*

38. Chairman Mao made this call to the nation's primary school pupils during the Cultural Revolution. The slogan later became a household saying.

39. Beginning in 1957, China's Party politics tilted toward the left, and then the ultra-left during the Cultural Revolution of 1966–67. Indeed, the two decades between 1957 and 1977 were the most violent in China's recent political history.

40. See p. x of Chu and Ju, *The Great Wall in Ruins*.

41. See the 24 November 1994 *People's Daily* (overseas edition).

42. The May 4th Movement, originating in Beijing and led by progressive intellectuals, became a national anti-imperialism and anti-feudalism campaign. The movement marks the beginning of China's contemporary history.

43. A traditional Chinese value that discriminated against women. The three obediences were, first, obedience to father before a woman got married; second, her obedience to husband after marriage; and third, her obedience to son after her husband died. The four virtues included *fude* (a woman's morality), *fuyan* (a woman's language), *furong* (a woman's manners), and *fugong* (a woman's work).

44. As a Confucian ethical ideology, the golden mean refers to a middle-of-the road attitude toward life, a denial of extremes in the negative or the positive, and a plea for moderation. Confucius says, "As a virtue, the way of the golden mean is the highest."

45. See Chu and Ju, *The Great Wall in Ruins*, 79.

46. See Pan, Chaffee, Chu, and Ju, *To See Ourselves: Comparing Traditional Chinese and American Cultural Values*. This fascinating study is the first to compare the dynamic and ever-changing cultural values of contemporary China and the contemporary United States. Surveying 2,000 Shanghai-area residents and villagers as well as 2,500 U.S. citizens from all points of the compass, the authors examine the extent to which traditional Confucian values have persisted in China despite massive governmental attempts to obliterate them and, similarly, the extent to which there has been a loss of "traditional" values in the United States. The result is a sophisticated yet readable account of the value systems of two complex and powerful national cultures.

47. The story can be found in the *Confucian Analects*.

48. The Gang of Four refers to Jiang Qin (Mao's wife), Zhang Chunjiao, Wang Hongwen, and Yao Wenyuan who were responsi-

ble for the atrocities committed in the name of following Chairman Mao's revolutionary line during the Cultural Revolution. They were all arrested and tried by a special court after the Cultural Revolution. Jiang and Zhang received a death penalty withheld for two years, Wang a life imprisonment, and Yao a fixed jail term. Jiang Qin later hanged herself in her prison cell on the outskirts of Beijing.

49. See Chu and Ju, *The Great Wall in Ruins*, 69.

50. Ibid., 70.

INDEX